101 New Pairs of Glasses

Essays on Perspective

And Why Seeing is Everything

By Elese Coit

101 New Pairs of Glasses

Essays on Perspective and Why Seeing Is Everything

Original articles published on www.elesecoit.com
© 2010, 2011 by Elese Coit

Now revised and compiled in twenty-six chapters.
Accompanied by brand new material from the author.

ISBN-13: 978-0936475103
ISBN-10: 0-936475-10-2 (pbk)
pp. 236
Includes Bibliography
SEL031000 1. Self-Development 2. Personal Growth I.Title

Las Brisas Publishing
PO Box 2987, Ventura, CA 93002
Printed in the United States of America

Dedication

To my readers, friends, radio fans, students, followers and clients.

To everyone who made comments, encouraged me to continue, challenged or just responded thoughtfully to my words on the blog and website.

In particular to the regular blog readers and Networked Blogs subscribers who followed the original series so faithfully. There were many days when I wrote just because you were there. When you liked or shared something I was encouraged to keep going.

Thank you so much for letting me into your life.

To my students and clients, you have made such a huge difference in my life – you encouraged me to reflect more deeply, you asked questions that had no answers. Your curiosity, your questions and your occasional suffering showed me that I too, needed to be willing to fail, to go out on a limb and traverse the small branches.

To my home-ies and my close circle, especially Mom, Dad, Cori, Tim and my daughter, you have been my dearest teachers. I made a pact with myself to live everything I teach to the best of my ability, day in and day out – you bore the brunt of that. I assumed you'd grow tired of my never-ending learning curve. How wrong I was. How lucky I am.

Because of all of you, my desire to respond to life's problems has continued to grow and led me deeper than I ever might have gone otherwise.

Author's Preface

In April 2010 I launched a blog series exploring new ways of looking at life.

101 was a random number I picked because I thought 101 days was a good amount of time to dedicate myself to writing. Little did I know the series would take just over a year to complete!

During this time I learned a few things about writing: to speak from my heart, to not stop, and to press the "publish now" button.

Anything beyond that is really gravy.

As it turns out, when I offered to create this book from the posts I'd published, so many people responded who wanted a copy, I then suddenly found myself with a high-priority writing project. I already had begun an autobiography, and had two other books on the go, but it felt important to get this out to those who wanted it and who had appreciated the blog series. I have included the links to the original blog posts so that you can still go online to comment with your thoughts and reactions if you wish.

One thing that concerned me as I began to edit this book was that my ideas had evolved a great deal over the course of the year in writing. I wondered whether my early articles would still hold water and whether I would even like them!

In the main I have. Where I have not, I decided to leave them pretty much as they were published. I have allowed myself a little editing for clarification or spelling and for the occasional emphasis. I've made author's notes at the end of a piece if further ideas arose in me that built on the original post in some way I felt was important.

I have grouped the posts into chapters by topic. The introduction to each chapter is new. These introductions pull together – not so much as a summary of the chapter that follows — but are what I might call digestive pieces. That is, me digesting my own work, sitting with it, reflecting on it, and seeing what came up.

I wanted these introductions to stand alone, to capture what came from re-reading my published work. These introductions also mean that those of you who have already followed the blogs have something new.

After each short chapter introduction you will find four or five articles. These are not grouped in quite the same way as they are on the website, where you can search by keyword. The keyword categories on elesecoit.com are still there and you will be able to search for the original blog posts on the website. However, the introductory pieces can only be found here.

Overall there has been a certain element of surprise in this process. Re-reading these 101 articles was a journey of learning something new, from myself. Often I had no recollection that I had seen or understood something as deeply as I had written about it. Sometimes things I struggle to articulate were laid out beautifully. That was very interesting. It points to the fact that we don't realize how much we know. The thinking mind is so busy trying to remember what it has heard or posturing to look good.

It is a paradox. As human beings we have enormous blind spots and yet despite them, wisdom flows through us irrepressibly. And what we need is always there in the moment when it's required.

In reflective mode, we are always teaching ourselves. We are always getting and creating new ideas out of nothing at all.

It serves to remind us that we are immersed in a bath of living wisdom. Even if we re-learn what seems like the same lesson, it is not the same, it is deeper and it is relevant to right now. I see no end to this depth. I see no limit to our infinite capacity to make withdrawals from the bank of fresh insights.

Whatever you call it, this human process of seeing anew is very delightful and ever so encouraging. It was what I was pointing to all along. And there it was again, 101 new ways of seeing, right in the middle of the editing process.

This experience has deepened my own humility and leaves me in need of acknowledging something that works through me but is not of me, which I render to. If I am very lucky I will continue to surrender to it forever.

With Love,

Elese

Acknowledgements

Michael Neill, my dear friend, you always make it look so easy.
You continue to inspire me every day.

Barbara Sher, without you this book would not be this book. You are awesome.

Steve Hardison, thank you for being so very clear.

Steve Chandler, you write so many downright good books. I intend to follow in your footsteps.

Sydney Banks, for demonstrating how anyone can wake up.

Anthony de Mello, I will never tire of hearing your wise lectures, "Wake Up To Life."

Joel Goldsmith, you will turn us all into healers.

Rachel Naomi Remen, MD, Byron Katie and Robert Holden, you taught me pure inquiry.

Bill Cumming, for being Love.

Greg Baer, for teaching Love.

George Pransky, for saying things I didn't understand but knew I could.

Ramana Maharshi, for taking my breath away.

A Course In Miracles, for challenging me.

Mary Baker Eddy and Christian Science, thank you for my childhood metaphysical training,
you gave me the bottom of the iceberg.

Jacob Glass and Debbie Ford, your integrity taught me what a teacher is.

The Center For Sustainable Change
Ami, Gabriela, Liz, Maureen, for the soul-sister connection and flying together in the unknown.

Table of Contents

101 New Pairs of Glasses

Essays on Perspective

And Why Seeing is Everything

Welcome to the world from the inside out.

Let the seeing begin ...

Preludes

We do not see the world as it is,
We see it as we are
Carl Jung

There is nothing either good or bad, but thinking makes it so
William Shakespeare from "Hamlet"

All we are is the result of what we have thought
The mind is everything
What we think ... we become
Buddha (563-483 BC)

Thought is not reality;
Yet it is through thought that our realities are created
Sydney Banks, The Missing Link

Advice and Good Common Sense

The Open Mind, Seriousity and Where Answers Come From

Is there anyone who, on any given day, doesn't hope that today they will find the answer to some issue they are facing? How can I have better relationships? How can I stop feeling so frustrated? What's the next step for me on my job search?

It seems too, that answers are everywhere. Billboards and commercial advertisements are offering us answers to problems before we have them. Our parents, friends, teachers and colleagues offer us answers to questions we ask and willingly give their advice based on learned life lessons or purported "greater knowledge." Other People's Answers abound.

The abundance of both questions and answers flying about the place makes it seems as if life is really a matching game. Get the question. Find the right answer.

I want to question this model of life. I'm suggesting answers don't exist until you invent them. And they don't exist until you understand what truly generates the problem.

We have lost the art of inventing and replaced it with the art of finding. They are not the same thing. To find an answer you need to be a good searcher, a good memorizer, or just a good follower. To invent an answer you need other skills: an open mind, lack of assumption, pre-disposition for adventure, not knowing and willingness to be surprised.

This is an attitude. A comportment. It's willingness to not take things personally. It's giving up on advice in favor of our own common sense. And it is more than that. It is the ability to see where answers really arise. Which is in us. But only always.

We all have the experience of how easily answers appear when we are feeling well in ourselves, listening with ease and not consumed with worry. It is also helpful to remind ourselves that there is really no limit on new ideas and that a new thought is possible at *any* given time.

A closed, know-it-all mind neither creates nor recognizes as many solutions and opportunities as an open, relaxed one.

But you already know this.

An Open Mind is a Beautiful Thing

Are you saying I might not know Everything?

There is a beauty in life that we are so in danger of losing — it is the sheer pleasure of an open mind. To be honest, my mind likes nothing more than a good answer.

Eldon Taylor[1] recently wrote:

"At a very early age we begin a process of conditioning. There are many facets to this process and its influence on all of us, and I have written about much of it. However, there is a particular form of conditioning that can set us up for disappointment and failure. I am thinking of the conditioning that teaches us we should have an answer. It's as though we are addicted to "answers" and need absolute answers to be happy."

I don't know if I am addicted to answers in order to be happy, but I may be attached to the idea that others will see me as a person who knows. That's an attractive proposition if I believe that what people think of me should form the basis for my life decisions.

I notice that enjoyment arrives through the open door of a "let's find out" attitude. Stress tends to dissipate. I see options and possibilities.

Many people who come to coaching do so for this very reason, because there seem to be a lot of closed doors and a dire shortage of exits. Opportunities don't arise to closed minds. So we use conversations to pry, wedge or gently nudge open — not the doors themselves — but the mind that sees only those doors.

If only we could see the parallel realities ... if we could see what doesn't happen because of our own attitudes and how things happen not for the reasons that we are quick to attribute.   A genuine not-knowing conversation sounds like "tell me more about that" or "how would that work?" or "why don't we try this and see?"

To have this kind of conversation you need to shift into inquiry and listening, and give yourself a big shot of willingness to not take things too personally.   These behaviors arise more easily when we are feeling well in ourselves and not consumed with worry.

An "I know" mind will never know as much closeness or find as many solutions and opportunities as an open one.

At least once today I'm going to say, "I don't know. Let's find out."   Join me if you like.

Author's Note
For more about the author of Mind Programming, Eldon Taylor (Taylor, 2010)*, see the Bibliography and resources section at the end of this book.*

Listen to the radio show I did with Eldon:
http://elesecoit.com/1/post/2010/06/demystifying-the-mind-with-eldon-taylor.html

Originally published as Pair #9 on 04/14/2010

To comment or read other comments online go to:
http://www.elesecoit.com/5/post/2010/04/an-open-mind-is-a-beautiful-thing.html

Dude. Seriously?

I'm dead serious

Sometimes I can take life so seriously. It is good to be reminded that it's OK to forget my persona and just enjoy myself.

When I think of all the energy I have put into things like a serious career, a serious relationship or even a serious wardrobe, I notice that time has a way of just gently correcting my perspective and putting everything in its rightful place.

None of these things really turned out to make differences in the ways I thought they might. I thought I could get a sense of self and importance that I could count on. Somehow. (How exactly did I think that would work?)

I am not saying there is anything wrong with gravitas, or any of these things I focused on. I rather have enjoyed my career, my relationship and my wardrobe. But were they serious? Uh, I don't think so.

Steve Chandler[2] is one of our faculty at Supercoach Academy[3] and his way of teaching our coaches to step forward into life and into powerful coaching so delightfully pokes fun at all the ways we take ourselves too seriously, that I can't help but review my life and wonder what the heck I was thinking.

Taking a moment to chuckle, just a little bit, at all the foibles I recognize in myself is a great way to be gentle and kind to me. Maybe I don't need self-love so much as a good sense of humor.

Originally published as Pair #36 on 05/22/2010

To comment or read other comments online go to:
http://www.elesecoit.com/5/post/2010/05/dude-seriously.html

Seeing the truth about education

If you want to really look at how our current educational system hampers human capacity, plus be amazed and learn something you won't forget, this is the best 11 minutes you'll spend today.

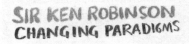

Sir Ken Robinson, world-renowned education and creativity expert, is a genius on any given day, but he's particularly swell when deftly animated by *RSA Animate*.

This animated video is adapted from a talk given at the RSA (Royal Society of the Arts).

I highly recommend this video on how the foundation of public education and the assumptions of mental capacity built into it have led to children struggling, attention deficit disorders, lack of creativity and an imperative need to change the entire educational paradigm.

Watch this on YouTube here: http://youtu.be/zDZFcDGpL4U.

My favorite quote from this talk is **"We should be waking children up to what they have inside of themselves."**

Instead, he says, we are "anesthetizing them."

His observations and insights on what is wrong with how we educate children is chillingly accurate.

And it doesn't have to be this way.

As Ken rightly says "We must think differently about human capacity."

Sir Ken Robinson.[4]
Bring on the learning revolution.

Author's Note
The RSA (Royal Society for the encouragement of Arts, Manufactures and Commerce) is a non-profit enlightenment organization committed to finding innovative practical solutions to today's social challenges. They can be found on www.thersa.org

Originally published as Pair #72 on 10/15/2010

To comment or read other comments online go to:
http://www.elesecoit.com/5/post/2010/10/losing-the-ability-to-think.html

You Are The Missing Link

Anyone round here seen my answers?

As I look around for guests for the radio show, I'm often thinking about what problems you, my friends and listeners, are dealing with. I like to think the shows might actually point to ways to solve the big problems any of us are facing right now.

Maybe that seems to suggest that someone will come along who has THE answer just for you...

and that would make me so happy!

I certainly do want you to find what you are looking for and yet the bare truth seems to be that no one else has your answer.

There is no direct link between someone else's wisdom or teachings and your problem. Or let me put it this way, the real link between your problem and the answer is not someone else's answer. It's you. It's the way you rethink the issue yourself, based on whatever information comes your way.

That's how I think it works.

Have you ever noticed that we often reject even very good ideas simply because we haven't come up with them ourselves?

Even if we specifically asked for them?

How many times have you suggested something to a friend and then they happily ignored your great advice, only to have them chirp later that they had this great idea (which sounded a lot like the one you gave them and they didn't want).

We really only want to hear our own answers and yet we are constantly looking for other people to answer our questions. (Did we learn this in school or what?)

But let's face it, between the good ideas of others and our day-to-day issues, all we can get is a good push in the right direction. And most of the time we resent that too.

Maybe we were just made this way. Maybe that's why we need to confront some of our problems over and over again, until we are ready to listen to our own advice. Until we are ready to take what we've gathered, make it our own and just trust what we are hearing inside.

That means the best advice you'll ever get might be someone who says nothing, but offers space for you to hear yourself.

Originally published as Pair #57 on 07/15/2010

To comment or read other comments online go to:
http://www.elesecoit.com/5/post/2010/07/you-are-the-missing-link.html

Awareness

Our Comfort Zones, Waking Up and The Lessons of Death

"We cannot say what 'awareness' is, but only what it is not." A. De Mello

Awareness is like a longed-for lover. When we don't have the lover, we imagine that when they come our life will be days of endless bliss. Then they arrive and not long after our joy is broken by underwear on the floor, hair in the sink and their forgetting to empty the cat box.

When we think of awareness as a state so elevated that we no longer experience the ups and downs of everyday life we are talking about an awareness that doesn't exist. We dedicate our time to seeking a mirage: a state of unbroken comfort, of no pain and no suffering.

We are missing the point. Awareness is not the cherry on the top of your spiritual hot-fudge sundae.

Awareness is the surgeon who has you under the knife.
Awareness is the mirror that relentlessly shows you yourself on your worst hair day.
Awareness is the truth-teller that won't shut up.
Awareness is the bully who grinds your face into the dirt.

To learn awareness is to fiercely participate in life in the raw. To reject nothing that might potentially show you yourself.

For me personally, awareness has come most memorably as I dangled at the end of my own rope. My own greatest learning happened in the afterburn of disappointment, disaster and destruction. These essays revolve around a personal question I asked: does awareness have to come via painful experiences? I don't have the definitive answer, but I know that pain does tend to wake us up.

These musings are about living in a willingness to let life have its way with me and me learning to remove barriers to being fully alive. I explore what it is like to stop fighting. I stop struggling to defend the idea I should know everything. I even stop fighting to wake up.

A bright light will jolt you out of the deepest slumber. Is it possible to recognize being asleep while still sleeping?

Don't touch that Snooze Button!

Wake Up Neo.

You know those moments when you "space out" for a bit? It just lasts a few seconds.

Imagine if that were your whole life! I have this horrible thought that I might wake up one day and realize I didn't have a life, just a lot of handbags. A life whose motto would be "I came, I slept, I shopped."

One of the reasons many people come to me for coaching is simply the horrifying idea that they might wake up one day and realize that Sam Walton's last words could be their own. Walton, Founder of Walmart, who died possessing enough riches to buy everything most of us could ever dream of having, and then some, was rumored to have said on his deathbed, "I blew it."

For this reason, I decided that my life would be about me coming awake and, to the extent I could realize this, sharing that possibility with others.

One of the books that nurtured my longing for more awareness and conscious action in my own life is Anthony de Mello's "Awareness."[5] Please put this book on your **Books To Read Before I Die** list.

De Mello was a Jesuit priest, a truthful, delightful, spiritual, and very frank man who challenged slumber and cared about all of us knowing that it was possible to live life awake.

He begins this book, which is a transcript of his lectures "Wake Up To Life" at Fordham University by saying, "we are born asleep, we marry in our sleep and we die asleep." Not a new idea. One that many other teachers would agree with and have also taught.

The horrifying aspect of this idea for me is that we can be asleep, but not even know it. Like in the film, The Matrix.

Watched The Matrix lately? It's interesting that first line:

"Wake up, Neo..."

Awareness for me is a kind of commitment.

It's a tough road, an amazing road, a never-ending road and the most worthwhile inquiry I've ever taken on.

Author's Note
I talk more about Awareness on this radio show:
http://www.elesecoit.com/1/post/2009/12/awareness-awareness-awareness.html

The show includes me introducing Anthony de Mello's four ways of taking action to come into greater awareness.

More on Awareness by Anthony de Mello (de Mello, 1992) *in the Bibliography and Resources section.*

Originally published as Pair #66 on 08/13/2010

To comment or read other comments online go to:
http://www.elesecoit.com/5/post/2010/08/dont-touch-that-snooze-button.html

Earthquake Widens Crack In Comfort Zone

Life is Short and That's an Understatement

The 7.2 Baja earthquake shook the house (and all of Southern California) and with lamps still swinging, moments later, I sat with my mother and best friend at Easter dinner.

Nothing like an earthquake to bring you back to earth with ... an instant refocus of priorities.

I'm not one to normally say grace at table but as I looked at both these people I so dearly love all I could think was, "I'm so glad you are here."

My guest Anne Perschel at Germane Consulting[6] talked to me on the radio about a woman who had found her abilities as a leader after a near death experience and tweeted "Should we recommend near death as a development experience?"

In the course of doing transformative work with people I've invited them to try a few things, but never that. Yet there's nothing quite like imminent death to whiplash us back to our senses. All at once we are open to a really big question like "If I die right now, can I say I've lived as I wanted to?" Suddenly unfinished business and procrastinated "I love you's" loom large. At the same time, all those squirmy ways we hid and ran away in order to avoid saying something that needed to be said like, "I'm sorry" seem ridiculous.

Benefits aside, I don't think I'll be suggesting a brush with death as a way to become intimate with what's important to you.

So, um, any extra weight to jettison before The Big One?

Originally published as Pair #4 on 04/07/2010

To comment or read other comments online go to:
http://www.elesecoit.com/5/post/2010/04/earthquake-widens-crack-in-comfort-zone.html

---

The No Tomorrow Choice

Get busy livin' or get busy dyin'

Today, not everyone made it. Suddenly or planned, freakishly or naturally, more than one person lost their life today. If you are reading this, you are not one of them.

It's well known that many people, when given a terminal diagnosis, have a very quick realignment of their basic values. Once we KNOW we don't have long to live, our desire to experience life intensifies.

We've all sleepwalked through a day (or months or years) at some point in life or another. We do that.

But if this moment is all you have, what is one thing that you know is important to you that you are not doing?

I guarantee you know what that is.

I'm not talking about changing the world. (But if you have a plan for that, be my guest!).

Maybe you just

- Start that book you bought?
- Call your Dad?
- Tell someone you love them?
- Finally sell that old car?
- Take one day off?

Each moment I have a choice. I don't have to make radical life-changing decisions every day. All I have to do is make a small choice, right now.

Quality of life is ultimately created by the choices we make, not the things we will have one day.

Perhaps ultimately the quality of an individual life is determined by our ability to make the choice to allow the present distraction to pass and the frequency with which we heed the urge to choose what supports our deeper desires.

Sometimes to choose to live fully now is to be willing to do the silly thing. I don't know what it will be for you.

But one thing is certain.

You may not be here tomorrow.

Nor may I.

That makes me want to look at my own choices.

Originally published as Pair #19 on 04/26/2010

To comment or read comments online go to:
http://elesecoit.com/5/post/2010/04/the-no-tomorrow-choice.html

---

Changing Yourself and Others

How We Change, Why People Are So Annoying and The Worst Job In The World

---

I'm holding myself hostage until you change

There is a reason why we say, "Hell is other people." As we go about our lives it does seem as if all our problems would disappear if people would just behave.

But all of the issues we have with other people are essentially cause and effect confusion. We are suffering from confusion of *source*. We are misappropriating the source of human feelings. We are failing to understand how internal trouble is generated.

As I drive my car and you cut me off, I fly into anger. My car passengers and I all agree: if I am angry it is because of what you did. There is no question, is there? I am clearly saying that my anger is coming from YOU and it will stop when you stop.

These essays are an exploration of the gaping hole in that pervasive and unquestioned logic called "the power of others to invade your head." I want to look at this. I want to see if it's really true. I want to explore the fact that we all actually know that it is not true.

Let's question the truth of the assertion that other people are the source of our own feelings. Let's question the idea that we need our anger in order to motivate ourselves. Let's examine whether we are really the emotional targets of those around us who we cannot control.

If I can't question these things, I live my life as an angry victim trying to change everyone and everything I come across that causes me a bad feeling. I'm going to try to change what I think is the source: people, places, things, careers, bank account balances. This is a painful way to live.

When I find myself thinking someone needs to change, I know that I've forgotten the truth about life. I'm confused. I'm lost. I fail to see the untouchable nature of my own inner life. Luckily, no matter what I think is happening, I can see fresh in the very next moment. I can see how life really works.

These essays are about becoming free. About learning to feel good when others seem to be making that impossible. About what we really control and what doesn't control us. About how nothing can get into us.

Does Anger Change Things or Just Piss You Off?

I'm unhappy, you're unhappy, sign here...

As someone who spent quite a bit of time supporting causes of all kinds, I can say I paid my dues to the "We're Fed Up And We Are Not Going To Take It Any More!" Club. If there had been an award points program for righteous indignation, I'd be a Life-Long Platinum Club cardholder.

So the Friday when the theme for the radio show was "Hot Pursuit of Happiness" it really hit me … I always assumed I needed to be unhappy about something in order to change it. In fact, the more angry I was, the better an activist I felt.

I was wrong.

It has not escaped me that we have not essentially changed much in any of the causes I campaigned for using my fists. That doesn't mean things haven't changed at all.

Women have more rights.
In some places gay people have more rights.
In some places you can now live without "being disappeared."

A picture of a starving child plastered on the news will still galvanize the sympathies and pocketbooks of millions of people for the right cause.

And we can do all of that, anytime we like, without any of the anger.

We can change anything we want without being sad, depressed or upset about it. We can do it because we want to. That's enough.

As my friend Jacob Glass[7] was talking about in a recent lecture: to teach happiness, we need to be happy teachers.

I think **to teach peace we need to be peaceful people.**

Jacob is right when he says that in the midst of devastation somewhere in the world, people are probably not wishing, hoping and waiting for "that angry, depressed guy to come back and help us out."

I know that I can be part of the solution to any problem anytime, if I want to and decide to.

I think we can change the world. One mind at a time. Starting with our own.

Author's Note
Jacob Glass is a teacher of mine who lectures in Southern California on A Course In Miracles. He can be heard on this show:
http://www.elesecoit.com/1/post/2009/06/jacob-glass-freedom-from-stressful-thoughts.html

A related article that may also interest you is "Hot Pursuit of Happiness."
http://elesecoit.com/1/post/2010/05/hot-pursuit-of-happiness.html

Originally published as Pair #33 on 05/17/2010

To comment or read comments online go to:
http://www.elesecoit.com/5/post/2010/05/does-anger-change-things-or-just-piss-you-off.html

My Operating System: 6 lines of code

You Show Me Yours, I'll Show You Mine

The last couple of days I've had a few of conversations about how I started my radio show and what my intent and core values are around it. I stopped to consider and I discovered a few things about our operating principles in life.

As it turns out, I have stuff I DO believe.

It's been very interesting to write this down and see it staring back at me. I recommend it to anyone. Writing down what I believe in gave me the chance to check my alignment. Do I operate from what I believe in?

The radio show and most of what I do, whether it is working with people or teaching transformative coaching in Supercoach Academy,[3] is all about seeing and teaching the true nature of change.

You'll not be surprised to find that my operating principles are focused on how I think change comes about.

Here are my six ideas on what change is and where it comes from:

- Personal change comes from thinking differently (not from anyone else's magic)
- People have everything inside them that they need already, there is nothing to get — not love or anything else
- Wisdom is what you hear when you clear the noise in your own mind (no one else's wisdom will do!)
- When we clear the noise we always know what to do next
- Teachers can share what they know, but only testing it for yourself will tell you if it's for you
- Daily life doesn't change if we don't apply teachings in practice in our lives

I am not suggesting these ideas are for everyone. In fact what is interesting for me is to notice how my life is built on them.

So I was wondering, would you like to consider yours?

What are some of your Operating Principles that lie behind your business for example?

What about your ideas of what creates a successful relationship?

When you have these, share them with me (or with someone you love).

Author's Note
Today I would add a seventh line of code:
- *In any moment you can have a brand new thought*

Originally published as Pair #12 04/17/2010

To comment or read comments online go to:
http://elesecoit.com/5/post/2010/04/my-operating-system-6-lines-of-code.html

---

No one is in there but you

How did you get into my head?

"There is only one way to happiness, and that is to stop worrying about things that are beyond our control." *~ Epictetus*

I was thinking about things that are out of our control. It reminded me of something that happened in my life that I hadn't thought about for a long time.

When I was 20 I had a stalker.

He wouldn't leave me alone and wouldn't leave my friends alone and would go to any lengths to find me. No matter how hard I tried to hide, eventually he would turn up at work or at my door. I became very frightened, and I remember vividly to this day what it was like to wonder whether I was safe, whether he would find me, whether something bad was about to happen.

A situation like this has many elements that are out of control. I couldn't have control over his actions, decisions or whereabouts. I also felt very little control in my own life.

Looking back on this event I know that I had very little understanding of my inner world and, even while I was taking action on the outside to protect myself, it took me a while to see and overcome the inner panic that I took with me everywhere I went.

And there is one piece of learning from this I cherish and would like to talk about today:

My inner state is mine.

It cannot really be disturbed by anyone or anything else.

When I fled the country to get away all those years ago, I wish I had known that I didn't have to take him with me in my head. That particular piece of the story took a bit longer for me to see. Now I know more about my own state of mind and the elements that play into how I feel within myself.

And, in the end, I'm very glad that other people can't actually step into our heads.

We do have to let them in.

Which means we can kick them out.

Originally published as Pair #89 on 04/23/2011

To comment or read comments on line go to:
http://www.elesecoit.com/5/post/2011/04/no-one-is-in-there-but-you.html

The Worst Job In The World

If Only They'd Behave I'd Be Fine

Wanted: one person who, against all odds, reason and the free will of other people will move all animate objects into positions that will, once and for all time, make everyone happy.

I know that sounds ridiculous; you know that sounds ridiculous.

So why are we doing it?

If you take only a few minutes to listen to a conversation happening near you I guarantee you it won't take long to detect all the directives, dictates and must-do's that we have for other people. They should call. They shouldn't call. They should get over it. They shouldn't be rude. They should be kind. They should get tough. And on and on...

Becoming the expert on what other people should do is a miserable game that one person always loses: you. But only 100% of the time.

In order to be Universal Project Manager In Charge of Making All Things Behave The Way They Should, we must ignore two basic truths.

One: we cannot change other people
Two: we cannot make other people happy – no matter what

Every time I think that someone needs to do something differently in order for me to feel better, I am ignoring one or both of those.

And who suffers as a result? Them or me?

The minute I ignore the difference between what I can control and what I cannot, I just signed up for the worst job in the world. It's the energy-depleting job of lining up everyone else so that I don't have to feel so bad.

I need to manage someone's anger so they don't direct it at me, so that I can feel better. I need them to seat me quickly at the restaurant, so I don't have to feel frustrated. I need someone to call me, so that I can tell myself they do care about me and stop worrying whether they love me.

It's a never-ending list of things to control.

No wonder we say "Hell Is Other People!"

People don't behave. Absolutely not. But we only suffer over that when we entertain that it is possible to manage them in a way that pleases us — instead of going to the source and just working where the real problem is.

I think we can all find one person in our experience we are truly convinced needs to change. But would you be willing to try, for one day, giving up trying to fix or control anyone other than yourself?

Resign as project manager of the universe for a day or more this week. Let others do their thing and you just do yours. If you have any aim, make learning how to feel good when other people seem to be making that impossible.

Hell is not other people.

Hell is the compulsion to change others so I can feel good.

Originally published as Pair #8 on 04/12/2010

To comment or read comments online go to:
http://www.elesecoit.com/5/post/2010/04/the-worst-job-in-the-world.html

You were expecting someone else?

Waiter, that's not who I ordered!

A special complaint place used to be allocated for moaning about other individuals — it was called the water cooler. Although that's now probably more likely to be the coffee room or the smoking area, figuratively speaking, we all have "gathered round the water cooler" with friends or colleagues to do some collective kvetching about people who annoy us.

A while ago a friend was telling me her particular complaint about a long-time customer of the place where she works. After a long story about what happened between them, the real complaint landed: "I would NEVER do that. He should not have said what he said." (Substitute: "they should know better" or "that's outrageous," etc.)

My response to her predicament was, "Oh, I understand. You were expecting someone else to show up in this person's body that day?"

The easiest way to be frustrated daily is very simple: Take someone and expect him or her to act or speak differently than they do. This recipe for you feeling bad will work with pretty much a 100% success rate.

Every time I have tried to control others I've failed. That goes for wanting them to *stop* doing as much as for loftier things like, wanting them to feel better. People do exactly and precisely what they want to do and that doesn't always please us. And frankly, pleasing us really isn't their job anyway.

If I don't like how someone is behaving, I either *Get Out of Dodge* or put a boundary down.

Right?

But let's be clear on what a boundary is.

A boundary is not a behavioral dictate to another, it is a clear statement about what can and cannot be done in my presence. It covers only the area I actually control. Me. I can tell if I have a boundary because I can enforce it on me – not them.

Although we know that we cannot control people, we still try to set boundaries "on" them (Don't smoke! Don't call me!). Then we proceed to complain that THEY make us unhappy. Which is the same as saying that if only they would just stop being themselves, we could feel fine.

That's a recipe for frustration. Give it up.

The only question we ever really face is not "How do I make them act differently?" but "How do I want to feel right now?"

When you know that, then you know what to do next.

Author's Note
Our need to change our internal discomfort by controlling the outside world is rooted in the fact that we do not fully understand how thoughts and feelings connect up. When we see we are hard-wired to feel everything we think, we tend to relax about changing and controlling others so much and what is right for us becomes much more obvious.

Originally published as Pair #30 on 05/11/2010

To comment or read other comments online go to:
http://www.elesecoit.com/5/post/2010/05/you-were-expecting-someone-else.html

Commitment

The Test of What We Really Want and Why The Easy Way Is The Hard Way

A Czech coach recently asked for a description of the English word "commitment." It seems that in the Czech language, there's no easy translation. How would you describe commitment?

Theodore Roosevelt said, "Speak softly and carry a big stick." A lot of us are using commitment as that "big stick." In other words, we tend to cajole, embarrass and guilt ourselves into doing things. Not where you should be in life? Feeling bad about not getting it all done? What you need is a dose of commitment! You can now punish yourself in the name of commitment.

I had a client who pinned her self-esteem on her ability to keep commitments. But commitment is not the gage of whether you are a good person. It is the natural result of becoming clear-headed about what you love to do and why. Commitment follows love like hummingbirds are attracted to red flowers.

If you've drawn a line in the sand as I have many times, you've discovered that your level of commitment dips and changes no matter how much you want something. To disapprove of yourself each time that happens makes no sense.

Commitment is not the measure of personal integrity, it is not even the deciding factor in getting something done, but rather the gage of our attachment to the outcome of a commitment making us happy. I'll say that slightly differently:

Low Commitment is a measure of how much we think something will bring us happiness. High Commitment is directly related to knowing that our happiness has nothing to do with what we achieve or do not achieve in life.

In the pieces that follow I notice that I'm tempted to think badly of myself when I'm not keeping commitments. I notice that avoiding commitment tells me how attached I am to achieving something in order to feel better. I discover that when I pin my happiness on achievements I tend to need a lot of structure to get where I think I'm going. I tend to try to rally up my commitment. But I am going about things backwards.

I have found that I have a great deal of natural commitment. I think we all do. It tends to show up as soon as I am not trying to force something to occur in order to make me happy.

Best Laid Plans Go Down The Toilet

Go On, Fawggeddaboudit

You know when you do absolutely everything to make sure that things go your way and then they just won't? It's as if all cooperative forces have left the planet and you are trying to restart the earth's orbit all on your own.

Let me be specific. For a few wonderful, adventure-and-delight-filled weeks, I was followed around the globe from New York to London by an Internet curse that would not allow me to consistently access the Internet and use my computer anywhere I went.

When I made this commitment to write and publish a blog post each day of the week I don't think the memo got round that I would really be needing internet access like, yunno, every day, on demand, all over the globe, thank you very much.

After a week of issues in New York and another few work days in London trashed by dropped connections ... I was left all alone with that little voice in my head insisting that the nationwide authentication fault on the UK network could be resolved with my own two hands if only I was willing to get really upset and make enough irate phone calls.

Thankfully there's the Other Voice.

It was asking "What are you making this mean about you...?" As I took a moment to uncover what I was telling myself I saw the headlines:

- I am not keeping my commitments (I'm bad)
- I'll disappoint people (no one will like me anymore)
- I could do more (I should be perfect)

I could see that without those judgments, it was OK to just do what I could and then stop being concerned about it.

I think very often we tell ourselves "there's nothing you can do, so don't sweat it" and that can be all it takes. We just walk away.

But for those times when it's hard to just let go and be happy regardless, it's useful to see the little horror movies we've got playing our heads. If nothing else than just to see how very silly we can be sometimes.

Originally published as Pair #55 on 07/05/2010

To comment or read comments online go to:
http://www.elesecoit.com/5/post/2010/07/best-laid-plans-go-down-the-toilet.html

Making a commitment certainly reveals just how uncommitted one is. Don't believe me? Commit to something. Recently I committed to writing a book. Several times actually. What happened?

"Dear Diary,

So far it looks like I like the idea of the book more than I like the reality of getting up at 5:30 in order to have writing be the first thing I do. BUT, I am very "committed" to my book.

Hm.

Having writing be the last thing I do is not turning out either.

But lots of nice, lovely wishful thinking happened!!

Loosely fitting it in writing time during the day between tasks is well, erm, not quite working out I notice. This book thing sure sounds good, but looks unlikely to happen if I continue like this ...

Do I or do I not want this?"

As I find with my clients so it is for me, the proof of whether we want what we say we want is tested by our willingness to do.

This is no doubt why, in coaching, asking someone to commit and just take the first step — actually works. At the very least you find out you don't really want it that much after all.

Having experienced the full effects of non-committal dilly-dallying, I decided I do want to write my book. And although I have decided this before and declared it, I am actually ready to be inconvenienced (get up at o'dark hundred) in order to do something I think is meaningful.

Commit Or Die.

It's me or them so ... the excuses have to die.

I just take one step: I set the alarm for 5 am so I can do some secret inner moaning for half an hour before I actually get up. (I'm only partly kidding about that). Then I create the page called "101 New Pairs of Glasses" and I begin.

Oh, look. Not dead yet.

Author's Note
Just over one year later, this book became a reality. The process was less about finding the formula or structure I needed to contain my work and more about listening and adapting myself daily to the form of work that my commitment wanted to take.

Originally published as Pair #1 on 04/05/10

To comment or read comments online go to
http://elesecoit.com/5/post/2010/04/first-post.html

If It Seems Pointless...

Hey, it's all dark in here!

The best recipe for misery I know is to compare your insides to someone else's outsides.

These are not exactly in the words Michael Neill[8] used when he first said this to me, but they were the words I couldn't manage to hear when I needed them.

Here is my salutary tale.

I was skimming through some great blogs on Huffington Post[9] and checking out Havi's[10] latest when my mind slumped down in the corner of my office in total misery.

Then my mind began, "Someone has taken my life and already written my book and is 20 thousand million times better than me and all original thoughts have already been taken." Suddenly (hardly surprisingly) all I wanted to do was go to sleep.

Funny how that is.

Anyway, I chose not to sleep.

Instead I went for a walk and petted a dog and when I came home I still wanted to sleep.

Again I chose not to.

I decided I'd just do one thing: One mindless thing.

This was not a good time to do something hard.

So I made a nice-*ish* dinner. Then I took one task that required zero energy and I did that. I noticed it wasn't so hard. And suddenly I was up and running again.

Sometimes, it's just taking the next step. The next mediocre, half-ass, stupid step.

Seems to work.

Author's Note

Only a few years ago it would not have happened like this. A thought of this kind could have sent me into a spin, affected my work and my self-esteem, and had me throwing away my writings and my commitments.

Today I know just enough about the nature of thought to know that when I am not feeling good I should not make big decisions, re-evaluate the purpose of my life and work, have important conversations or use sharp knives.

Originally published as Pair #47 on 06/08/2010

To comment or read other comments online go to:
http://www.elesecoit.com/5/post/2010/06/what-to-do-if-someone-steals-your-life.html

Commit. Whatever you do.

That's a definite Yes. I think...

For me, one of the great values of putting something into the same brain compartment where you store: "pick the kids up from school" and "catch plane home" is that when you've really committed to something, you find out if you really want it or not.

What a relief.

Everything that follows the moment of commitment is information to you about how much you really want something or how much you don't.

Sometimes, it's the first time you actually realize you really just don't want this thing — and can stop fooling yourself (or trying to please others or not let them down) and just get on with your own life the way you want to live it.

We can waste a lot of time trying to "should" ourselves into things we never wanted in the first place, just like those college majors we dithered over.

Commitment is the great sorting hat!!

May you not end up in Slytherin.

Originally published as Pair #70 on 09/13/2010

To comment or read comments online go to:
http://www.elesecoit.com/5/post/2010/09/commit-whatever-you-do.html

Control and Powerlessness

Who Really Has The Power, How We Sap Our Power and Trying To Rule The World

The opposite of powerlessness is not control. It's knowledge.

None of us have to look very far to find some area of life where we feel we are at the mercy of others. It might be your boss in your case, or politicians, or the economy and the world at large. It's not difficult to see why we feel powerless, frustrated and drained.

But what if we could see our own role in making ourselves into victims? In this chapter I explore our level of control in life. I see how excuses and blame make me into a victim. I notice how refusing to be loving until other people fix themselves makes me into their victim.

There is something basic to understand about just how much we really are in charge and what exactly we are in charge of. I always thought damage, weakness and victimhood were the inevitable result of life's hard knocks. Then I noticed that only I could carry my own past everywhere I went. No one else did this for me. This was a revelation.

It showed me I had failed to understand something basic about the nature of power and control. It was a simple failure to understand that no one else has control of the inside of me.

I had missed one important fact: we all feel whatever we think.

To be powerless, to be a victim of life, is not to know that. It is to live unaware of our own thoughts — even as they come alive through us daily. That's powerlessness. That's victimhood. The attempt to control others in any form is always the result of this fundamental missing piece in our own understanding.

It is as mistaken and misguided as me going to the Doctor and saying, "Doc, I'm sick. I need some help."
Then him replying, "OK. I have just the cure for you. I'm going to prescribe this pill here for your neighbor."
"Thank you Doc," I'd chirp, "That makes me feel much better!"

Beware the cult of victimhood. It promises lots of medicine for your neighbor and ignores what you really need to know to fully come alive.

Make An Excuse, Make A Victim

Excuse-Free Zone

An excuse is a thief of self-love.

It steals your life away from you and robs you of your power.

Why? An excuse always explains who you are being by attributing your behavior to an outside entity. It says you are this way because of something: your partner, those drivers, the calendar that didn't have the correct meeting time or perhaps, stress.

When you make an excuse you are creating a victim out of you.

And being a victim feels awful.

Recently I had a look to see the role that excuses (and complaints) play in my life. I put myself on an excuse fast, and as a result I now have 101 essays sharing ideas with you.

So if you'd like to play along, see if your little thief comes in the form of excuses, complaints or criticisms.

See which one is your default setting – the place you always seem to end up.

- Do you have a hard time saying No, without giving an excuse?
- What about requests – do you make requests with or without complaints?
- Are you excusing yourself while asking?
- Do you give lots of reasons for why you can't do what you told yourself you will do?

How about apologizing – ever had the yucky experience of someone trying to say they are sorry while making an excuse about how it's SO not their fault? Bleuch.

If you can see this will be a useful for you to experiment with, here is a challenge:

For today declare your life an "Excuse Free Zone" or a "Complaint Free Zone".

What does that mean?

You are on a total, 100% Excuse-fast. No excuses. Ever. None. Nada. Zero. Nil. Never. For the whole day.

Rules:
1. No excuses. (Do no complaints if you prefer – but don't do both!)
2. Notice how it is for you as you go.
3. No beating yourself up.
4. Pick a specific start time and a specific end time too.

Originally published as Pair #2 on 04/06/2010

To comment and read other comments go online here:
http://elesecoit.com/5/post/2010/04/make-an-excuse-create-a-victim.html

Stop The World I Want To Get Off

Honey, Where's The Remote?

Ever see the film "Being There" with Peter Sellers?

Sellers plays an innocent, older man who is a live-in gardener in a large home. Chancy, his character, is pictured as a simpleton and you get the sense he is not quite all there in many ways ... but it is impossible to dislike this gentle man.

Clearly the people he works for think it best to shelter him from the world, so his sheltered life consists of tending plants within the walls of the compound and watching television – which he adores. This is all he knows.

Until one fateful day.

When the elderly owner of the home dies, the house is sold and Chancy is forced to leave the estate walls he has lived behind his entire life.

The scene in the film when he walks out the front door and up the road with a suitcase in one hand is wonderful. You realize immediately that the house, a beautiful estate on the inside, is situated in a very, very run down part of town.

As Chancy makes his way down the road he not only encounters the world for the first time — he walks straight into the ghetto and it's not long before he's confronted with a rather mean-looking bunch of men.

Here's roughly what happens next.

The men begin to get more aggressive and distinctly menacing and as the pitch rises, Chancey is on totally unfamiliar ground.

Threatened, lost, and in the middle of a potentially dangerous situation, Chancy does the only thing he knows how to do: he reaches in to his pocket and pulls out ... the TV remote. He points it at the men, and then presses the button to change the channel.

When the world is not how we would want it, and people do not behave as we think they should, isn't how we react very much the equivalent of hitting the remote and hoping for the best?

Originally published as Pair #21 on 04/29/2010

To comment or read other comments online go to:
http://www.elesecoit.com/5/post/2010/04/stop-the-world-i-want-to-get-off.html

A dollop of helplessness to go with that...?

One of the weirdest things to comprehend, as I've become a student of the mind and how it works, is how we create our world through our thinking.

But **what is it to "create our world?"**

The popcorn version of this idea says that you "get what you think about" — which interpreted literally means: parking spaces, Porsches and bicycles appear just because we think about them enough.

Now if you can do that, great. That makes me very happy.

But if you've tried to *think and make it so* and that did not work — here's a clue. Change the words "get what you think about" to "experience what you think about."

We experience everything in the world through our thinking about it. I don't experience you; I hear, see and experience my thoughts about you.

That makes sense. In fact, it's incredibly simple and boils down to:

It's hard to have a good moment if you are having shitty thoughts.

The implications are just a simple, and just as far reaching. If you are in the middle of something and you want to experience something different, you will have to change your thinking about it.

Of course, you can also walk away.

Well, quite right. And you can walk away and continue right on thinking about it too. For as long as you like. Even for a lifetime, if you so chose. You will continue then to produce that experience for yourself in every moment of your now.

The simple maxim that you get what you think about = you are experiencing life through your thoughts about life. If you are aware of that, then you have choice.

The definition of powerless is not realizing that choice.

Author's Note
I don't advocate that you get very busy and change your thinking or try to rid yourself of certain types of thoughts.   You would fail. No one who is alive has stopped thinking completely or controlling thought before it arrives. The hyper-vigilance required to monitor thought, is alone, enough to keep you deep in thought!

Try reflecting on this mind-bending and radical fact: that we are always, no matter how much it looks otherwise, feeling our own thoughts. And that is ALL we feel.

Originally published as Pair #68 on 09/06/2010

To comment or read comments online go to
http://www.elesecoit.com/5/post/2010/09/whos-got-the-powerlessness.html

Decisions, Indecisions and Discipline

Finding Our Own Way and Life Without The Multitasking Maze

Fact-sifting is a common way to navigate through life. Yet reliance on logic alone for direction can and does create strain. After all, even with all the facts at our fingertips (rarely the case) we cannot know the future and we cannot predict all good outcomes always. So the brain, even with all its power cannot reliably steer us to the best-case scenario 100% of the time.

Pointing to the limits of logic some might suggest that instead we rely on the heart for steerage. I think we have so little experience of heart wisdom that we tend to confuse it with sentimentalism and emotionalism. I've seen as many people also go astray by following their every emotional zig and zag as those who've misjudged on pure logic. So what to do?

In one corner we have feeling-based decisions, on the other, logic-based decisions. Which one do you think is more highly prized in today's society? Which do you use most?

In this chapter I explore a third way. Let's call it "natural intelligence." Something within us that we can use to know what is right for us in any given moment.

This is neither a brain function nor a purely sentimental one. Some refer to this as the gut. Others might call this intuition. Whatever you call it, I see very few people actually using it.

You can recognize this natural intelligence In yourself because it is always accompanied by the presence of calm, clarity, and a sense of peace. And an absence of stress or anxiety.

For example, the more concern I can feel in myself about a decision or course of action, the more I know to hold back and wait. I know I'm not in touch with my best information source. I am wary of my ability to make a good decision when I can feel conflict is going on within me.

To navigate by internal wisdom is to experience a feeling of clarity within. That is my sign to move forward. It has taken me some practice to learn to be un-influenced by confusion as it screams ACT NOW! Only the tempest in me shouts, "Don't just stand there, DO something!" This is the worst idea ever. Doing is no substitute for clarity. Don't just do something.

Guidance by internal compass feels naturally good to all humans. It is a relaxed and comfortable but an alert, active and clear state of mind sometimes also referred to as "the zone." You can trust it to flex, respond and re-direct you to your best course of action — if you can learn to recognize when it is present and when it is not.

A peacefulness follows any decision, even the wrong one. -Rita Mae Brown

Here is the square root of our daily stress: Decisions.

We agonize at length over pros and cons, we have mind-maps and "Why Trees" and 9-step models that help us over-cook the decision making process.

Even decisions that don't have huge impact will be whirled through the endless spin cycle of yes/no/maybe/do you think...?

Did you know that studies have shown that it is no more effective to ponder a decision than to simply pick based on first impression? It's about 50/50. In fact, according to research Mark Tyrell turned me onto,[11] "many decisions you are better off not thinking about it."

I think we have so much trouble with decisions because:

We have turned the decision-making process wrong way round: toward ourselves.

We think the biggest impact of a decision will be whether we turn out to be right or wrong, rather than realizing that some decisions don't matter that much, some are reversible if you get them wrong and most are not life threatening.

We are petrified of getting it wrong.

Plus, **we have a tendency to think our decision scorecard is the mark of our intelligence.**

Our fear of feeling bad and looking bad to others is paralyzing.

Western society prizes logical abilities and in general gut feel gets relegated to the sidelines only to be brought in in a pinch or a last resort after all of the avenues, fallbacks, consequences and pitfalls have been examined and exhausted.

It's worth looking to see if drawn out, over-thought decision-making is causing you sleepless nights or taking up lots of your mental space.

The mind was meant for greater things than data analysis and endless agonizing.

Author's Note
You can hear my radio show on decision making here:
http://www.elesecoit.com/1/post/2011/05/easy-decision-making.html

Originally published as Pair #91 on 05/20/2011

To comment or read other comments online go to:
http://www.elesecoit.com/5/post/2011/05/easy-decision-making.html

The Rock And The Hard Place

Decisions, Decisions, Decisions

Do you experience stress when making decisions?

I've been thinking about the decision-making process and there are two things I notice:

One, that the stress is highest while we are thinking about the need to decide and Two, the stress disappears as soon as we make a decision.

In short, the time we most suffer is during the time we are feeling our own uncertainty.

So I've been testing out two ways to do uncertainty: Being unsure and taking action (forward movement) and being unsure and not taking action (stasis).

We are always in one of those two places. I can't see any in-between.

To illustrate: Let's say you are in uncertainty about whether or not to stay in a relationship with someone. If you date someone and you are not sure they are right for you, but don't break up with them — that would constitute being unsure but taking no action.

Here's the odd thing, though, no matter how often you repeat, "oh, I don't know what to do!" what you might notice is that actually, a decision has been made. Until you leave, you've clearly decided to stay. For now.

Given this, I think perhaps what frees us up is not the moment that we finally make the cut one way or the other, but is the clarity to notice and to understand that the decision is already there in some form, we are just thinking that it is not and experiencing the thought of uncertainty.

In actuality we are constantly making new decisions...

... but not really realizing it. Each day we decide again. And again. And again.

Decisions are only right now. Not forever.

Noticing this also does something else, it reminds us that we have the power and that each moment is new.

We are actually making decisions all the time in this way. We answer the phone, we don't, we order one thing and not another. Where does this information come from? The deciding process?

Byron Katie[20] used to confuse me when she'd say, "I don't decide to stand up. I look around and I notice I am standing." It took me a while to see what this meant.

Here is how I finally got what she was talking about.

Sit down and then try to make your body stand up *by using your power of decision* — by deciding to move each muscle you that need to use in order to stand.

What happens?
Where will you begin?
Which muscle will you consciously need to decide to move first?
What happens if you decide to move a different one?

In the end we are in a constant state of internal decision-making and it's easy to see the choices we've made by looking at where we are.

The nice thing to know is that we can chose again, right now.

Nice to see reality.

Originally published as Pair #35 on 05/20/2010

To comment or read other comments online go to:
http://www.elesecoit.com/5/post/2010/05/the-rock-and-the-hard-place.html

Anti-Disciplinarianism

Discipline is the new dirty.

We love it, we hate it and we don't need it. But let me come to that in a moment.

We associate discipline with the ways our parents forced us to do things because they "said so." Or we talk about it as if it were a missing gene: "I dunno what it is but I just can't stop…"

How many times have you argued that what you really, really need is more discipline in order to get things done? Discipline is our special form of self-coercion exacted viciously in order that we might do, not just our chores, but also the things that we say we **want** to do.

This is curious.

And totally wrong.

Why would you need to force yourself to do something that you say you want to do? (Or force yourself not to?)

Well, you don't.

Recently I heard someone say "I really want to exercise, but I just don't have time." So I asked them to take the word "exercise" and substitute it with "pick up the kids from school." (Then I practically had to duck and cover, but that's another story).

The truth is we will do what we care about and what we commit to, and we don't need discipline to do it. We will simply find the time. Somehow.

How do we do that?

I did not pick up my daughter from school everyday because I had previously given myself a very nasty dressing down and swore I would not reward myself if I didn't do it. I simply arranged life to get there.

I did it because it mattered to me.

If you are not doing something (especially when you say that you are committed to it) it is because somewhere inside you have not decided that it matters enough. Making something matter is a decision. I had to decide that it mattered to me to write these articles. On a Sunday night, ready for sleep, I may have to remind myself why it matters.

And I need a deeper reason than hating myself if I don't.

Next time you want to do something, try NOT punishing yourself into it. Try finding one positive thing about what you say you want to do that connects you deeply with why it matters to you. (In other words, you do not get to use: "He won't speak to me if I don't," or "I'll hate my body forever.")

If you can't find a positive *why* for you, then you will never be able to disapprove of yourself enough to force yourself to do it. Not in the long run.

Author's Note
Here are a few more resources that relate to this chapter:

Your Brain Doesn't Care What You Think
 http://elesecoit.com/2/post/2010/02/why-your-brain-doesnt-care-what-you-say.html

Rick Hansen on the radio for, Change Your Brain, Change the World
http://elesecoit.com/1/post/2010/03/change-your-brain-change-the-world.html

Why Your Brain Doesn't Cooperate with Lindsay Brady
http://elesecoit.com/1/post/2010/02/why-your-brain-doesnt-cooperate-truth-about-the-mindbrain-connection.html

---

Originally published as Pair #7 on 04/11/2011

To comment or read other comments online go to:
http://www.elesecoit.com/5/post/2010/04/talking-nasty.html

The Price of Multitasking

Have you ever walked into the kitchen, opened the door to the refrigerator and then stood there wondering what you came for? Welcome to the club.

Our ability to Focus, or not, was my topic for one of my radio shows and it was a good one.

One of the discussions that came up repeatedly in a recent training was how could what I teach help people to be able to focus and yet to still be able to **do lots of things**?

It is as if we think that focus will slow us down somehow. That we won't get enough done if we stop rushing around. So we think it makes sense to work on focus while we rush around.

How focused do you feel as you rush around?

Isn't that precisely when you are more likely you leave the house and forget the lunch you packed?

I often hear people say that the solution to getting a lot done is to learn to multi-task better. Many times I've had clients tell me, "my problem is I'm just not that good at multi-tasking."

We look with envy at others and their ability to be super-soccer Moms that juggle kids and high-pressure jobs. But should we?

On Yahoo recently people were talking about how AMAZING Obama is at multi-tasking. As one put it, Obama was simultaneously dealing with "*Birth certificate/Trump, Bin Laden, was in Florida for the shuttle launch … spoke at the Correspondents Dinner, gave speeches on the budget, went on Oprah, all in the last week*!"

I doubt that President Obama is managing all of these things on his own or that his ability to keep the country ticking over is down to his great "multitasking" but still, look at how we love and revere the multitasker!

We imagine they are jetting from place to place while tapping into their iPad and signing up new business on the phone from a seat on an airplane all while writing the next great American novel and managing their children's homework via our revved up, multi-device, superhero lifestyles.

We are down on ourselves when we are not doing the same. We can't see a way out that is any more profound than just getting more done. Yet we also intuitively know that when we are overloaded our work is poor quality, we become more forgetful and we are actually more likely to need to repeat what we've done or redo it.

Ever regretted pressing that SEND button in the rush of trying to get through the inbox?

Research has long pointed to the fact that the human brain only processes one thing at a time. Recently studies at Stanford[12] are showing that our ability to pay attention, use memory and switch from one task to another is deteriorating.

So where is our adoration for multi-tasking coming from?

Is there real evidence that multi-focus is the new fabulousness?

We would do well to look beyond the anecdotal evidence that multi-tasking is good.

Which is the better measure of our productivity, doing a bunch of things poorly, or doing a few things well? You don't have to choose, but if you did, which seems better to you?

What I want to suggest is that when we have true focus, we do tasks well, enjoy them more and complete them fully with fewer mistakes at a natural pace.

Let me suggest a few simple measures of whether or not you are using that kind of focus.

Here is what being focused feels like:

- good
- connected
- creatively juiced up
- clarity
- time irrelevance
- completion

Here is what multi-tasking feels like:

- rushing
- behind the eight ball
- strain
- tiredness
- clock-watching
- doing over and over

Which would you choose?

Author's Notes:
Here is the link to listen the show on Focus
http://www.elesecoit.com/1/post/2011/05/how-to-focus.html

I also recommend listening to "Focus On Demand" with author Tom Sterner (Sterner, 2012)
http://elesecoit.com/1/post/2011/01/focus-on-demand-with-tom-sterner.html

Originally published as Pair #90 on 05/06/2011

To comment or read other comments online go to:
http://www.elesecoit.com/5/post/2011/05/the-price-of-multi-tasking.html

Flops and False Starts

Growing Pains, Getting Started and Giving Up

Although we get many lessons in life, one of the lessons we fail to learn is that it's OK to learn our lessons.

We have the false idea that once we learn something we won't make a mistake ever again, or that we won't need any more lessons! Many people put themselves under terrific performance strain, imagining that they need to be able to dance before they ever hear the band playing.

The truth is that we almost never feel ready for what life calls on us to do – whether it is taking the new job or becoming a parent. To assume the new roles we will take means being apprenticed to the unknown for the whole of your life. Many of us hate and try to avoid mistakes and failures. Successful people learn to be learners and to appreciate lessons, even if they come in the form of mistakes and mishaps. Even if it takes a while to get the message.

Look at any human on this planet. We were born ready to learn. There is nothing we need to improve about ourselves in order to accomplish this. Every skill required for this task was bundled into the human toolkit long ago.

Let's give up on the whole correlation that feeling unprepared for something is the same as being inadequate. It's not. Life has never once given you more than you can handle, or you wouldn't be reading this. We are petrified of failure, but our only true failure is our inability to fall flat with a sense of humor and perspective. In fact, you have had disastrous failures you thought you'd never survive and somehow you have already picked yourself up and moved on. The question is what did you learn?

People tell me their dreams to speak French, to sail round Cape Horn, to create a charity for a good cause and in the next breath they'll say, but … "I have no time," "I don't know how" or "I can't." What they mean is they don't want to look funny or disappoint people. They hate to fail as if it were equivalent to being stripped naked in the public square. That's not naked; that's human. Are you willing to sacrifice your deepest longings to keep your vanity unblemished?

There are no perfect conditions in life. But we were made perfectly to live life. We can thrive with no preparation, no readiness and no time if we are willing to be someone who learns.

Unready for Readiness

Recently I was responding to a Yahoo! Forum post from someone waiting to be in "the best place possible" before they got started with a project that was important to them.

It made me think … as we embrace new challenges timing and readiness are important, but

there is a difference between being in the best place we can be and being in the perfect place.

To be in the best place in me means actually caring for myself well and showing up fully. In other words, I'm aware of what is going on right now in front of me and am more focused right here in this minute than either in the past or in the future.

When I am present in this way I not only know what to do but also what not to do. I know what I am ready and not ready for.

When I am waiting to be in the perfect place, well, that's it isn't it?

I'm waiting.

I generally feel I'm not up to the tasks in front of me. That they are simply too big and I am simply too small.

I think I have to be something I am not in order to live my life.

I forget that clearly I am enough to live my life perfectly well. The proof of that is I'm here.

The moment I start wobbling around thinking there is something I need to fix or some "better place" I'll arrive at one day — be it a place of greater understanding, a place of less ego, or a place of less stress — then I am saying I need fixing before I can live.

Sometimes we'll use up a whole lifetime like this. (Know anyone who's been getting ready their whole life?)

While I believe it sounds like a good idea to do things when we are ready, what I notice is we also find lots of ways to tell ourselves we are not ready yet.

Today I'm reflecting on just how much our "not ready yet" can cost us.

And perhaps, the world.

Originally published as Pair #6 on 04/10/2010

To comment or read other comments online go to:
http://www.elesecoit.com/5/post/2010/04/are-we-there-yet.html

Setting your own green light

Over the course of my life I've given in to defeat many times. I've given up.

The thing I noticed is that I am often walking a finer line than I think on this, because giving up never feels like throwing my hands up in desperation and sinking to the floor in a heap: it feels more like simply not getting around to something.

Giving up sneaks up upon us in insidious forms like simply not making time and putting things off until tomorrow.

Last week I was noticing how many times I heard people say, "life just got in the way," as the reason why they didn't do something they said was important to them (like writing that book).

But how does that work?

Can life really insert itself between your fondest dream and your daily calendar?

I just don't believe life gets in the way. I don't believe there is no time. I believe we never take the time to choose.

We too easily consent to wasting our lives on details. We spend little time on what's important, much less even on prioritizing what's important.

I also don't agree that the reason we give up is because it's scary or too hard.

On a basic level there is an unwillingness to train mentally. Or maybe there is just too much tolerance for our mind's own wanderings. We consent to a reactive state of helplessness, which gets us out of the task at hand, but kills our longer-terms dreams.

Hearing our own answer to this is important.

I've noticed for myself that a way out can be to engage others in our game and not allow myself to work alone, to disappear, or to become the victim of my own lazy thinking.

You can hire a coach to help.
You can start or join a group.

Having spent a week with a group of fellow writers, I notice that it shifted something for me to join up with committed comrades.

In our group we all encouraged one another. We all admitted where we were blocked and then took a step together. We set the timers for 45 minutes and then said, "Go!" And we worked.

At any point in life there are a multitude of choices and for most of us in this writing group, we could each clearly see two paths ahead: one involves making some hard choices, the other allows me to lag behind and then ultimately to give up and blame it on life, the kids, work, and being just too busy.

Which to choose I wonder?

Author's Note
I always find it interesting when experts share methods or techniques that work for them and then I try the very same thing and it doesn't work! I am wary of having anything in this book sound like a solution or prescription for you when it is no more than my experience. What's valuable is not what others do, but the reflection, observation and listening in which we come to see our own individual answers. Your ability to recognize what's right for you is worth more than 1,000 expert solutions from other people.

Originally published as Pair #53 on 06/23/2010

To comment or read other comments online go to:
http://www.elesecoit.com/5/post/2010/06/giving-up-is-the-easy-part.html

On Doing What You Love

Do What You Love and The Math Will Get Easier

One of my proudest moments was the day I got a call from my daughter to tell me she was completely changing life direction.

"I've thought about it," she said, "and life is too short to **not** do what I've always wanted to do."

The decision to switch focus means that school will take longer now. She has to start over in some respects. But there was so much passion, clarity and excitement at the decision that I felt an immediate surge of happiness within me.

I recognize this as the feeling of unconditional love for another person; it happens when all you want is their happiness.

It was only later that I noticed something else, something even more significant.

As she heads further along this path, the love for what she's chosen to do has literally infected everything and not only is she enjoying the required classes, but describes them as "easy."

And yes, we are talking about math.

Now somehow I don't think they lowered the math standards. What's going on, I think, is that doing what you love changes the context you are working in and therefore changes your experience of whatever is in front of you.

If that's true, then it has to be true for anything:

You will experience whatever is in front of you depending on what you bring to the situation.

You can try this out by consciously deciding what you would like to bring to any situation. You can decide to make your next commute "joyful" or your next laundry day "magical" and see what happens. This is one of the great learnings I had from my coaching with Bill Cumming.[13]

When I made a long commute recently — I spent the drive looking for ways and reasons to enjoy the scenery and relax. My mind collected all the information it needed to be content with things and minimized the rest. I just overlooked it. Often we say we can't overlook things. But we most certainly can. We can decide at any moment what to make important. I find it fascinating how this works.

And the repercussions, if you really consider this, are vast.

Originally published as Pair #11 on 04/15/2010

To comment or read other comments online go to:
http://www.elesecoit.com/5/post/2010/04/on-doing-what-you-love.html

Taste The Flames

Avoid getting scalded by life?

My Dad is the author, Lee Coit, (Coit, 2010)[14] and he told me this story about himself as a small boy...

He was getting the usual lecture you get as a kid. You know the one that's meant to keep you from burning yourself on the stove? It's the "Don't touch! That's HOT" admonition. You know, the one that is delivered with a good finger wagging.

Later he was sitting next to fireplace and his mom, my grandmother, is giving him very serious instructions to NOT go near the fire. Because, that's **hot**.

No sooner did she finish her last words, my father stuck his hand right into the flames.

"Why did you do that?" my grandmother asked.

"Because I wanted to see what 'hot' felt like," he said.

We think that the more we understand or know, the easier life will become. But what we mean by "easy" is that no more bad stuff will happen.

We soon find that...

no matter how much you know, how enlightened you are or how spiritual your life, bad sh*t still happens to you and all around you.

In fact, one of the questions I get most when I'm coaching people is "I know so much, how come this is still happening?"

But the point of living is not to never experience hot.

In fact, as my Dad proved, you really have to have your own experiences of hot, cold and everything in between — because no one, no matter how knowledgeable, can ever give you the experience of your life.

You can only get that by living it.

Here's is my favorite explanation for how this works:

Becoming more balanced and aware does not mean that bad things never happen, it's that when they do, you know you will be OK.

Originally published as Pair #82 on 02/28/2011

To comment or read other comments online go to:
http://www.elesecoit.com/5/post/2011/02/taste-the-flames.html

Feeling Good, Being Authentic

Genuine Achievement, What's In You, Good Advice and Going For Discomfort

Which would you chose – feeling good or feeling yourself?

While every human I know would choose feeling good over feeling not-good, very few understand the true ingredients of good feeling. Some think they're supposed to be "up" all the time and work hard to feel great and be positive. Most are not managing this all that well. Others make feeling good into a vacation home that they visit in the summer and hope to live in permanently one day.

Meanwhile, all kinds of cravings take over in us due to our aversion to even brief moments of boredom, discomfort or bad feeling. This life of trying to find the magic formula for feeling good is like swinging on an eternal swing without ever having your feet touch the ground.

We are missing ourselves. Have you looked at you lately? Did you get a hint of who you really are or did you see only your criticisms and unfinished self-improvement projects?

You may notice that at times when you forgot yourself a bit or neglected to remember you were on the self-development path, how a nice feeling might have just been hanging around. It's interesting how good feeling is utterly un-caused. If we could all see that how we'd relax! We'd stop running around trying to get to elevated states and avoiding low ones.

We have our microscope focused on lack, imperfection, fear, failure and aging bodies! We assume we are broken. We don't even register the thousand natural urges to reach out, to help, to send love and to care. Where did those come from? Who taught us how to feel love? No one. We just know. So who is this self that knows? This self is not messed up. You may mess up at times, but that is not the same thing.

The more we know our genuine selves the less feel-good-drive we have. Good feeling pours out of us because it's our nature. The more we know genuine desire, the less we need to acquire and the more we want to express. The more you know your authentic self, the less you need to get rid of "feeling not-good," and the more you find yourself feeling just fine.

There is no need to put pressure on to feel any particular way. We can just relax and feel ourselves. If you've no idea how that feels, now is a good time to begin.

The Real Me. Really?

Hey, leggo of my Ego!

There are not many things we would all agree upon, but most of us seem to agree that it is a good thing to "be yourself."

Well, this got me thinking. What does it actually mean to "be myself?"
What does *authentic* look like?

I spent a week hanging out with the delightful Robert Holden[24] on his Coaching Happiness Course in London, and one of the things we explored in depth was the distinction between the self that we construct (our persona, or what Robert calls our "learned self") and the self that simply *is* (some might call that the unconditioned self, the true self, or the real you).

Just about every self-development course I know has something to say about these two sides of a human being — the real and the constructed. In fact, the appeal of self-development is often the promise that we will discover our authentic selves. But what does that mean?

Too often it means nothing more than trying to improve on ourselves by ridding ourselves of an ego. This is based on the idea that the authentic self is the ego-less self.

Now that may be true on some level, but I am not at all sure I need to get rid of the ego before I can experience who I am.

In order to know the real me, I think I just need to relax and stop thinking I need to be different.

After all, most of us have had a lot of self-improvement done, but would we know our authentic self if it turned up in the mirror one morning?

As long as we keep thinking that the authentic self is perfect (and we may get there one day) and the ego-self is bad and needs to be got rid of we are in a terrible, terrible bind that prevents us from recognizing who we are at all.

What if the real you does not need any more self-improvement in order to turn up?
What if rather we just need to relax and be more accepting of all the sides of ourselves in order to experience who we are, really, right here and right now.

Originally published as Pair #56 on 07/12/2010

To comment or read other comments online go to:
http://www.elesecoit.com/5/post/2010/07/the-real-me-really.html

The bravery to be average

We love to celebrate achievements and successes, but sometimes I wonder if our champagne-fueled trophy ceremonies celebrate a lone winner, cheered by a crowd of self-punishing people who either feel bad or jealous that they are not the ones on the winner's podium.

Underneath it all, we onlookers are aware of having set high sights on goals and having failed to reach them. Maybe we were miserable and humiliated. Sometimes we turned that failure into the lifelong drive to never feel that sting again.

Once we set a course toward destination **Avoid Failure At All Costs**, we pay a high price.

Two things happen:

We lie to ourselves about who we are
We try to be something we can never be: a perfect human

We lie to ourselves because we tell ourselves being perfect is possible, which it is not. We tell ourselves striving for perfect works to create perfection. Which it does not.

Then we abandon ourselves.

We walk right out of our own bodies when we think that it's possible to be anything other than who we are.

That doesn't mean accepting mediocrity. Who said the only choices were perfection or uselessness?

To achieve something feels good. Anyone and everyone is capable of achieving all sorts of things. I consider it a great achievement that I started my own business. But it gets a bit nuts when I try to be a perfect businesswoman.

I made a promise to myself that every month I'd keep my accounts up-to-date and every time I do that and keep my commitment, that feels good. There's nothing wrong with that.

I notice that doing what I say and living up to what I believe doesn't require me to be perfect. Just to live and be myself. Maybe living as myself actually requires that I mess up, otherwise how can I even know my own preferences?

We don't need to make what we are perfect, that is just another form of self-punishment. You can't self-punish yourself into loving yourself. And you can't do well in life if you don't care for yourself. So you might as well let it out and be you, warts and all. Who else are you going to be?

This week ... consider rewarding yourself for doing a terrible job.

You might notice that you are still yourself — perfectly acceptable You.

Originally published as Pair #69 on 09/09/2010

To comment or read other comments online go to:
http://www.elesecoit.com/5/post/2010/09/dare-to-suck.html

Genuine Desire? Or Faux Fear?

What I'll do to feel good, and what feels good to do

The first quarter of 2011 has passed. I sit down and reflect. I think about what I'm grateful for, I take time out from busy-land to visit and spend time with what is meaningful to me.

One of the mistakes I've made in life is not taking the time to just have a fireside chat with me. Or rather, the me I'd like to have show up in my life. Lately, I have some questions:

What would the me who's not afraid like to do?

What would the me who knows she is safe like to try out?

What would the me who is pure enjoyment like to express?

So often I've looked at my life from the point of view of what I assumed was possible, probable, feasible or within reason. Or simply what would make me feel better …

… instead of looking for what wanted to come up from inside me and get out.

And the more I look the more I seem to know one thing.

I know how to tell the difference between what is my authentic desire and what I tend to do to try to alleviate my worries and concerns.

Genuine desire feels different. It feels good. And it feels good whether I think I can have what I desire and whether I consider that something *feasible* or not.

And that's way different from doing something in order to feel better.

One month ago I made a commitment to write an autobiography. I made a commitment that I've kept relatively quiet as I nurtured this very personal desire to do something that has more to do with expressing what's inside me then trying to be something or write a book in order to not be disappointed with myself.

This is a totally different process.

I decided to write the most self-honest account of a life and to share my stories and my learning so openly that anyone could draw their own insight and healing from them.

And here is the thing about a genuine desire. It came paired up with total commitment.

If you've ever tried to commit to something and failed (and I committed to this book many, many failed times!) then you know how gruff that experience is.

And I'm here to tell you it probably wasn't an authentic desire.

The measure? How you feel about it.

If you sit back to reflect on your progress at some point, and on what you feel committed to, see if you are able to discern the difference between:

What I do because it feels good to me.

What I do to me to try to feel good.

Originally published as Pair #85 on 03/28/2011

To comment or read other comments online go to:
http://www.elesecoit.com/5/post/2011/03/genuine-desire-or-faux-fear.html

Going For Discomfort

Just Get Me Out of Here

I was talking to Freeman Michaels[15] about how we relate to our bodies and how one of the keys to this, but also to life in general, is **developing a new relationship with discomfort.**

That seems very true.

I can see many distractions, cover-ups and excuses I've created to paper over being uncomfortable with discomfort.

For example, if someone you care about is going through a hard time, you might definitely want the situation to end or for them to feel better, right?

Someone I know is going through what most would call a pretty grueling divorce. I notice that rather than listening I am in problem-solving mode. My position, even as I try to be supportive, is really saying: "This is hard for me to watch."

How unhelpful! This is my discomfort showing.

I want to give true support and love. When I consider how I would really like to be, what I would like to say is how much I trust that they will get through it, that things will be fine, that I love them just the same, that there is good in everything.

But that doesn't come through when I'm lost in self-concern and problem solving. That's not listening!

When we reach the point of discomfort and we feel the panic and discomfort rising — be it in a yoga pose stretched to capacity, standing in front of the pastry counter with sugar cravings reaching a peak, or listening to someone giving us honest feedback — all we want to do is make it stop.

Rarely do we consider that we might very well survive this moment. Period. Even by doing nothing but standing in it (much less by actually deciding to move toward it!).

In many self-growth practices this idea of moving toward pain is called learning to "be with." Hospice workers learn it thoroughly. It is a quiet and yet difficult art to master in many ways.

For the rest of us, those not highly trained in being with people giving end of life care or acting in emergency situations, it can be a shock the first time we try to *step toward and not away*.

Learning to "be with" is one of things I can really suck at sometimes.

So ... how do I want to be with the part of me that wants to be rid of that part of me that really sucks at this?

Author's Note
Two radio shows may interest you in relation to this topic ...

Freeman Michaels can be heard here on releasing weight:
http://elesecoit.com/1/post/2010/07/its-not-about-the-weight.html

My interview with Stan Goldberg on learning life lessons by being a hospice worker:
http://www.elesecoit.com/1/post/2009/09/lessons-for-living-without-regrets.html

Originally published as Pair #63 on 07/30/2010

To comment or read other comments online go to:
http://www.elesecoit.com/5/post/2010/07/going-for-discomfort.html

Taking My Own Advice

Put up and Shut Up

I keep a few sticky notes around my desk to remind me of what's important to me.

You see, sometimes my mind doesn't really remember the bigger picture, the higher purpose or the wider context of my life and so I've just installed instant recall of my own simple truths.

Most of these notes are from my personal learning and insights, like "everything is for good."

Others are nuggets of wisdom that I'd like to learn such as "communicate with a request or a promise." All of them are within quick glance so that if I am rushing or have a tough day, I have these sanity grabbers.

A few weeks ago I put a new one on the monitor right in front of where I set up my laptop. It was the focus for that day and it said:

"FOCUS: *Be Even More Helpful*"

Today I walked into the office and before I picked up the phone for my first client call I took a pen to that particular sticky note, added a colon, and just below

"Be Even More Helpful:"

I added,

"Shut Up."

Originally published as Pair #39 on 05/26/2010

To comment or read other comments online go to:
http://www.elesecoit.com/5/post/2010/05/taking-my-own-advice.html

---

Forgiveness and The Past

Trying to Get a Better past, Being Human and Ticking Clocks

The past always teaches us the same lesson: "It's over."

Strange, isn't it? If you really think about it, everything that happens to us has this very neat, absolute truth to it. It's gone.

The fact that it's gone does not stop us thinking about it. On the other hand, neither is there a compulsory reason to continue thinking about it. An event and our thinking about an event are two different things. Knowing this helps us in a few ways.

One, it makes it possible for the bygones to be bygones. You can actually leave things in the past. In fact, that's where they actually are, if they are anywhere at all.

Two, you actually cannot bring anything into your present unless you think about it. The only way to get anything into NOW is to bring it here – by thinking about it.

Three, thoughts change all the time. There is nothing about the nature or content of the past that can change the very fact that thoughts flow. Thinking is always changing. Right now.

This must mean each of us is thinking and each of us is always in a new now. That makes nonsense of the idea of having a future to get to and a past to leave things behind in.

I find it incredibly helpful to see these basic truths about all humans. This loosens our ideas about the grip of the past and the "sins of the past." It frees us to see fresh and literally "think again." After all, it really is over.

Before I finally learned this I kept the past alive by bringing it forward and playing it to myself. When I saw that my past and everything in it was old news – I began to live.

Then I also saw something deeper. I saw that if these facts were true then not only could I forgive what happened to me, but I could also relax about being a human being and see how my own thinking was leading me around by the nose.

And as for my worries about the future ... the more I saw that it is one great big Now changing moment by moment, the more I realize there is literally no tomorrow.

I came to life.

Get a Better Past

Stop Looking Back, You'll Only Hurt Your Neck

There's no doubt in my mind that it's possible to create a future that is nothing like the past.

It's not actually that long ago that I could not see that at all. In fact I was down on all fours in my garden in my London home, in agony. My future had gone down in flames. My past, come back to haunt me.

I had just lost someone I hoped I'd be with for the rest of my life.

He left me. (Yes, I **did** believe in princes, white horses and someone coming to save me!).

Those of you who know this story already know that I reached a point when I looked back and all I could see was failure behind and failure ahead ... this massive loss was just one more in a long string of failed relationships and one person at the center of it all: Me.

I knew in some way I had to be the problem even though I wanted very badly to blame the person who had just abandoned me, and all the others before him, right back to my own father.

My Dad and I have a great relationship today but for many years I treated my father badly because he divorced my mother. Even after therapy I had very little peace and I seemed to be on auto replay.

Everything I'd tried up until that moment was more like an attempt to try to get a better past, than a step to create any real and lasting ability to move myself into a new future.

I have to tell you that what changed life for me was to decide to actually commit to personal change and to hire someone to help me.

I had a series of wonderful personal coaches / teachers who had a profound impact on my life. I hired the wonderful author and coach Michael Neill[8] for two and a half years. I changed.

Then one day, I had a flashback on my old life: I met someone who had a similar job and a similar relationship pattern and I remembered my own moment of surrender and the fork in the road that I took that day in the garden.

I knew without a shadow of a doubt I made the right decisions to stretch into the unknown, to invest in myself through coaching, reading, meditating and questioning my own assumptions about life — then to absolutely leap into all that has made possible.

How very important that has been.

More than I could ever measure.

Author's Note
The Bibliography and End Notes of this book contain all the references to the works and teachers who have had the greatest impact on me in the last decade.

Originally published as Pair #14 on 04/20/2010

To comment or read other comments online go to:
http://elesecoit.com/5/post/2010/04/get-a-better-past.html

Hey I'm Only Human!

To err is human, to forgive is human too

I can give up the idea that one day, if I work hard enough, nothing will bother me, I'll never get upset or angry and I'll never again have a unkind word for myself or others.

Sigh

No matter how much personal work I do I can still come up short, get lost in a petty idea, and do not follow my own best advice.

Just today I was upset and frustrated.

The funny thing that really hit home about this was that I was angry because I thought I shouldn't be frustrated. I thought I should be able to "do better than that."

To come nose to nose with my lack of humility was a jolt.

Did I really think I was so self-aware that I should never have a problem or find anything difficult ever again?

The truth is I got upset that I didn't have my sh*t totally together. And it got me thinking:

What does it mean to do personal work?

Do I really believe that it means I'll grow out of myself?

Where in the fine print does it say, "After a certain time has passed, you will no longer react at all and never make another mistake?"

There's nothing wrong with not being able to cope, getting frustrated or just plain losing it.

Which reminds me of this wonderful quote:

Every human heart is human.
   -Henry Wadsworth Longfellow

How unhelpful to think that one day we'll become so wonderfully self-aware that we will crawl out of our humanity.

There is nothing wrong with being human.

In fact, it's rather divine.

Originally published as Pair #62 on 07/29/2010

To comment or read other comments online go to:
http://www.elesecoit.com/5/post/2010/07/hey-im-only-human.html

No time to wait for death

Death reminds you to think about who you need to call

They released Rod's ashes to the sea.

I've never attended a ceremony like this and I'm not sure there is anything quite like a surfer's memorial, when your buddies paddle out together, form a circle and release their friend's ashes into the water.

I didn't know Rod. But as I watched six of his surfing friends on the water and more onshore who considered it a privilege to have known Rod, it reminded me how there is no guarantee you'll be here tomorrow. I was thinking...

... we have this notion that when death comes knocking we'll have plenty of time to answer the door, pick up a few things along the way, grab our hat and coat, kiss the dog.

But I actually want to be complete with my life in each moment.

So much so that if I miss the knock and whoosh, I'm just suddenly gone, I've taken care of all my resentments and grudges. I've made peace. Today. Right now. The legacy that I want to leave is that people in my life know I love them. No one is left wondering.

Sorry, no time to make a will.

Got to make a few calls first.

Originally published as Pair #73 on 10/29/2010

To comment or read other comments online go to:
http://www.elesecoit.com/5/post/2010/10/no-time-to-wait-for-death.html

Freedom

Out of Your Head, The Freedom of NO and Human Life Support

If what binds us is our own illusions, that means we *are* free

There is a direct link between our thoughts and our physical senses. It helps to learn this, not so we can become thought-manipulators, but so we can enjoy living in a world we understand, rather than tilting at windmills, full of fear and confusion.

Here is my definition of freedom. It is not, as most people say, to have enough money in order not to worry anymore. That's not freedom. Freedom is to understand how life works!

I liken not knowing how the system works to living in Oz, where everyone is under the illusion the great wizard is wise and real but behind the curtain there is nothing but a man and a microphone. Most of us are under the illusion that we already understand how our own world of Oz functions, so we run around trying to escape the witch and believing wizards will make us free. No one is free in this scenario, until the veil is lifted.

Whenever I don't see the unfailing link between what I am thinking and how I am feeling, I am missing the stairway to freedom. When I overlook this connection, I am certain that my feelings are coming from other people and from events around me. I dive into misguided action. I go on a vigorous campaign to change others. And when I fail, I assume that the reason is that I did not find quite the right pressure point or the right incantation. So I keep looking for another way and I may never pull the curtain back and look behind it. This chapter is about doing just that.

The instant I see that all my feelings come from what I am thinking in that moment; I am free. I am free because I see the system and I know how it works. My illumination is instantaneous. If I misunderstand the thought/feeling connection, it looks as if my feelings have come from someone or something other than myself and I'm deluded again. Who can I change, what pill can I take to dispel my own illusion?

Would you like a failsafe method for dissolving your illusion? Simply wake up and see that you are the feeling-maker. You are just like Dorothy, who had the power in her all along.

When that unmistakable experience of clarity hits you, you may well notice a strange thing: you are already free.

Four Ways Out Of The Box

Multiple Personality Success Disorder

I spoke with Eldon Taylor[1] on the radio show and there were so many things I loved about our show that it is really hard to pick, but let me share his **four keys to becoming self-actualized.**

Before I give you those, if "self-actualization" rings odd for you, here's the idea:

The point of exploring the inner self and how we work mentally is so that we can express who we are rather than rehearse who we think we need to be.

When we don't understand how our own cogs turn we are little more than organ grinder monkeys. We are still dancing to someone else's tune; we simply learn how to get lots of bananas.

To understand this is the beginning of the way out. It is also a theme in my work.

This week is not the first time one of my clients had a realization about this too. He saw that very little mattered in life if he couldn't be himself while living it.

He called it "Standing for Who I Am."

When I saw that same truth for myself, I knew I didn't want to spend the bulk of my life managing my personalities and masks (work, home, mom, athlete). It was a complete turning point in my life.

While it's possible to have success without going to the trouble to reconcile the different parts of yourself or understand your own inner world, this has always smacked of very empty success. It is to arrive at the pinnacle and then not recognize the person who is looking back in the mirror. Perhaps not even like them so much!

That is not all that satisfying. It is certainly not a very meaningful definition of success in my book.

So, here's the four-point plan from Eldon:

1. Guard against what goes in
2. Get inside yourself
3. Change the context
4. Remember you are a miracle

Author's Note
If you reflected on point 2 alone I imagine it would lead you to all the rest and probably much, much more.

Listen to my show with Eldon Taylor here:
http://elesecoit.com/1/post/2010/06/demystifying-the-mind-with-eldon-taylor.html

Originally published as Pair #50 on 06/12/2010

To comment or read other comments online go to
http://www.elesecoit.com/5/post/2010/06/four-ways-out-of-the-box.html

One of the things I've learned to do in the last few years (with some practice) is to identify some of my "stinking thinking."

I've learned to discern better when I am hitting me with my own stick.

Let's say I feel a bit tired, it's nice to tell the difference between real physical exhaustion and the kind of tiredness that comes from whatever I am thinking. Or repeatedly thinking.

When we are telling ourselves things like, "oh, no, not another day with more to do that I'll ever get done!" it's not all that surprising that our physical bodies feel sluggish or that we have an overwhelming desire to go back to bed — or just not get up in the first place.

I've often encouraged my clients and students to do exercises that help them to distinguish thoughts that precede feelings as a way of experiencing first-hand how their own feelings and thoughts are linked. And how they experience that link.

If you are doing any thought monitoring (watching thoughts come and go or any exercise that has you be aware of thoughts as separate from you) you will have noticed how useful that can sometimes be to increase your overall awareness of the very nature of thought.

However, we thinkers can start over-thinking our thinking.

For example, a true fear response or gut reaction will not need observing or processing. Nobody needs to analyze his or her thoughts about a house fire, "Hm, I wonder if I should leave now? It is interesting I'm having that thought!" We simply rely on a flight-or-flight response to get the heck out of the burning building right now.

Equally, with peaceful thoughts. How much thinking about that do we need? They feel good. They arise. There's naturalness to them. That's good enough for me.

Checking in with thoughts can be as quick as asking, "Is this really true?" Or it can take some examination, "Now, what was the thought that was just before this feeling of ... X." But we don't want to get lost in the examination itself.

The usefulness of any such practice is not to make us consider everything we think and be in analysis all the time, but rather to get more deft at connecting how feelings arise from thoughts rather than things.

For me all of this helps create greater awareness of the link between thoughts and feelings.

Awareness means more choice. And more choice means more freedom.

And I like that a lot.

Author's Note
I don't believe that you need specific awareness practices in order to see the connection between thoughts and feelings. But you will always benefit if you take time to reflect on how you see this connection playing out in your own life.

Originally published as Pair #42 on 05/31/2010

To comment or read other comments online go to:
http://www.elesecoit.com/5/post/2010/05/get-me-out-of-my-head.html

---

How to Say No

I'll Like Me If You Will

I wish I had a dollar for every time I didn't say no when I really wanted to. And I also wish I'd known a lot sooner in life that ... the key to saying no is permission.

If at any time I am having trouble saying no, here is what can help:

- Give myself permission to want what I want
- Give myself permission to not look for a reason why
- Give myself permission to be wrong (Are the planets likely to grind to orbital halt?)
- Give the other person the right to hate me (They have the right to feel how they feel, I get to do the same)
- Give them the right to say no

People want things. I want things. If we really accepted that everyone simply wants what they want and feels how they feel, based on what they are thinking at the time, it opens the cage door and frees us all.

In the end, one can be liked, or free.

Author's Note
More on the difference between loving and being a doormat on this video from Greg Baer
mms://67.199.127.39/video/topten/topten10.wmv

Originally published as Pair #45 on 06/03/2010

To comment or read other comments online go to:
http://www.elesecoit.com/5/post/2010/06/how-to-say-no.html

Life, but not as we know it

Recently, I had a glimpse of **the profound kindness of our human life-support system**.

You know how on a music player you have the LOOP button? After the song finishes it loops back to the beginning? And in the scientific field, you have "closed systems." We also talk about "feedback loops."

I spent a day with George Pransky[16] and one of the things he talked about was how thought and feelings truly are a looped. We have only to look to our feelings to know exactly the quality of our thinking at any given moment and we have only to have a thought in order to have the feeling that goes along with it.

So ... if it's true that thought-feeling is a completely closed loop then it can never be true that *things create feelings in us*. It is always our own thoughts that set off our feelings. Our thoughts are solely responsible.

That means we are living out our thinking through all of our physical senses. We are literally, thinking our way through life.

And all this means that we have been beautifully constructed.

How incredibly smart it is that we each came equipped with an infallible GPS system that would always help us if we ever get lost and forget what's what.

If we are always feeling the world through our considerations about it then when we feel bad or scared or afraid maybe it is not because a scary world has bumped into us.

If "scary" is generated inside me, the world around me may have no inherent meaning at all. Period.

It could be just a simple blank canvas.

As I open up to the possibility that *the world is neutral then it can become a terribly kind place to live* and not only that, but while we are here, how kind to have been given a built-in navigational device to help us find our way. What a gift.

I used to believe that how I felt was telling me that a bad thing was happening to me but now I understand that the only thing a bad feeling is telling me is whether the quality of my thinking is dropping or rising.

Which ultimately means that Shakespeare got it right "Nothing is good or bad, but thinking makes it so."

Author's Note
There are a few books to take you deeper which I highly recommend spending time with …
Sydney Bank's "The Missing Link" (Banks, 1998)
George Pransky's Relationship Handbook (Pransky, 2001)
and Mandy Evan's[17] book "Travelling Free: How to Recover from the Past by Changing Your Beliefs" (Evans, 1990)
All are listed in the Bibliography Section and wonderful resources for breaking down limiting beliefs and gaining a greater understanding the nature of human thought.

Originally published as Pair #96 on 06/20/2011

To comment or read other comments online go to:
http://www.elesecoit.com/5/post/2011/06/its-kind-to-be-human.html

Goals

Butt Kicking, Going For It and Just Plain Losing It

Would you be willing, for a moment to consider a goal that you have? Would you now also be willing to take a quiet moment to find the deepest reason you can find for why you have this goal?

Perhaps you have never lifted the hood and had a really good rummage round underneath what you hope your goal will get you. Maybe you, like me, accepted that by definition it is good to have a goal or several goals and it is not good if you don't have any.

Start unpacking all the various preconceptions about goals and you may well find that at no point is there the option of having no goals at all. It is almost inconceivable that in our success-driven world we should allow such rudderless-ness. In fact, there is a special insult reserved for those who don't have goals in life: drifters.

But is it true that without a goal you would be set adrift aimlessly on the sea of humanity?

To think that we need goals in order to move forward in life is to be mistaken about our nature. In this section I explore some common myths about goals and some radical reinterpretations of our assumptions about what would happen if we dropped them.

I am not suggesting that we need to drop them. I am interested in getting to the bottom of them — and indeed anything that suggests that we need *something* in order to be fulfilled and happy, or assumes we are lazy and broken. I'm wary of anything, even spiritual things, which ask you to adopt signposts, must-do's or frameworks as preconditions for living fully.

I've seen beauty arise out of the most unexpected chaos. I've spent years pursuing useless goals meant to make me happy. I no longer assume the need for planning, control and motivation in order to make myself do something. If I need goals to get going, it's highly likely I am doing something I've no business doing. When I am clear-headed and inspired goals seem to spring out of me from nowhere and come to life. In fact, often when I've thrown away my goals I have far exceeded what I was previously struggling to achieve. The magic arrived.

Perhaps each of us can only discover the rightful place for goal setting once we realize that nothing needs to be added to or subtracted from human beings in order for us to thrive.

Butt Kicking

When you reach for the stars will you need a boot in the backside?

What's the best way to get your goal?

Do you need a drill sergeant wielding a clipboard, a score sheet and a loud whistle?

Or do you prefer to ease into success with a cup of tea, a pen, a blank notepad and an appointment-free morning?

I'm featured on Kristin Noelle's[18] video kaleidoscope on the fine art of self-motivation affectionately known as "butt-kicking."

The whole series is 20 minutes long, so here's my bit:

http://elesecoit.com/video-blog.html

Originally published as Pair #93 on 06/09/2011

To comment or read other comments online go to:
http://www.elesecoit.com/5/post/2011/06/butt-kicking.html

The Going For Nothing Goal

Go On, Go For Nothing!

Many spiritual paths make **getting enlightened** a goal.

The trouble with this idea is that, barring having a burning bush experience, it sounds like a very long and arduous path to getting somewhere you are not entirely convinced exists.

On the radio show with Peter Fenner[19] we talked about how you can be totally fulfilled without changing anything at all. That sounds so far off reality for most of us that it's easy to just pass it over completely. But the more I thought about it, the deeper the implications.

It made me consider the last few years of my life when most of my effort has gone into personal change. I could really identify with the thoughts I often had that went something like...

- *I need to create a "better me"*
- *When I understand more, life will become easier*
- *If I get better at this stuff, I won't have any more problems*

Sound familiar?

Those of us who are either pursuing personal change or teaching it, what would happen if we actually called off the search?

One of the implications of Peter's view of loving what is (and which those of you who read and follow Byron Katie's [20] work know) is that the only time we suffer is when we are arguing with reality.

The result of loving things as they are with no need to change them is, in fact, peace. "When you argue with reality, you lose," as Katie would say, "but only 100% of the time."

The idea that there is *nothing to become* underlies the effortlessness and accessibility of the Buddhist nondual teachings of Radiant Mind.

Here are some of the things you can learn from Peter in his book "Radiant Mind" (Fenner, 2007):

- the anti-frantic environment
- how to stop making a problem out of having problems
- why we get stuck when we think there is more to know than we know right now
- why we don't have to make anything better

It is also my experience that painful thoughts and feelings dissolve when we are not struggling to establish what needs to change in order for us to feel better.

I had such a wonderful experience of sharing this state of awareness on the show with Peter that I think just listening to it, there is a very good chance you will feel the truth of what he is saying.

Here's to a taste of what it is like when there is no goal to get anywhere!

Author's Note

To hear Peter and I talking on the radio show about non-dual awareness go to:
http://www.elesecoit.com/1/post/2010/04/totally-fulfilled-without-needing-to-change-anything-radiant-mind.html

Byron Katie explains how to do The Work on this powerful show "Who Would You Be Without Your Story?"
http://elesecoit.com/1/post/2009/07/who-would-you-be-without-your-story-live-with-byron-katie.html

Originally published as Pair #16 on 04/22/2010

To comment or read other comments online go to:
http://www.elesecoit.com/5/post/2010/04/the-going-for-nothing-goal.html

No More Goals!

What do goals and ice cream have in common?

People tell me the hard part about goals is not setting them, but the pain of not getting them.

I think the hard part is not confusing the goal with our happiness.

Most of us define a goal as something we will get or become.

But why decide you want something you don't have and then pin your happiness on getting it? It's like deciding you want ice cream and forcing yourself to be miserable while you drive to the store to get it.

One of the worst things we can do is decide that getting a goal will mean finally being happy, successful or worthy. It doesn't. You are already worthy no matter what you do and whether or not you ever get your goals.

A goal is just a clear picture of what "there" looks like. It's neutral. Getting it or not getting can be neutral. Unless you pin your happiness on it.

Personally, I have enjoyed having goals sometimes because I can see and envision where I'm headed. For me right now, that looks like a book rather than a tub of Ben and Jerrys, for example. I know that I will be able to recognize "there" because I'll have a book in my hand.

But let's not get confused.

Putting together a book (and this is true of any goal) is a bit like putting together a very large puzzle. The stepping-stone goals are like the pieces of the puzzle: the more of them click into place, the more I can see what the final puzzle looks like. In fact the more pieces I click into place, the more the final puzzle solution (the book) becomes *inevitable*. A no-brainer.

At no point do I want to get frustrated that my puzzle isn't finished yet and toss over the table. That's no fun. That's not enjoying the game. I want to enjoy the process of putting together my puzzle. Piece by lovely piece, I want to relish seeing the images and forms come together, as if by magic, out of a pile of mess from an upturned box.

I want to be happy doing my puzzle and happy not doing it.

Because I don't ever want to confuse puzzles, or ice cream, with who I am.

Author's Note
This radio show explores the unknown as a place of possibility
http://www.elesecoit.com/1/post/2011/07/living-in-the-unknown.html

Originally published as Pair #76 on 01/09/2011

To comment or read other comments online go to:
http://elesecoit.com/5/post/2011/01/no-more-goals.html

Save your procrastination for the important stuff

I have wanted to write a book for a long time. About 40 years actually. Now that I'm finally in the process of writing it I'm fascinated by what has changed in me that flipped my switch from "one day" to "right now."

What happens in any of us that is **the critical difference between doing something and not doing it?**

I'm not talking about getting in the groceries or finally changing the battery in the smoke alarm, I am talking about why we procrastinate on anything that is really important to the heart and soul.

After all, that's what we save our best procrastination for, right? For me, that was writing a book. So I'm reflecting ...

- **What flipped my switch from Talker to Doer?**
- **Why is it that now I have an accountability group?**
- **Why is it that now I have goals I'm setting and exceeding without effort?**
- **Why is it that I'm not struggling to keep promises?**

Here is what I notice that is different.

One, I really do like (enjoy, want, genuinely desire) both the end product the process of doing it. Just because I do.

Two, I enjoy being engaged in something in my life that is meaningful to me. *I've worked out that the other way is not all that great.*

Three, I know that I am able to feel good whether or not I ever write the book. No matter what.

Of all these things, here is what else I notice. One and Two are not new; Number Three is.

I know that doing what you love is more fun. I know doing what you love is meaningful.

I just never knew how to feel good about my life without a condition of some sort. I'd agreed with myself I'd feel good when I was successful. I'd feel good if I was in a great relationship, etc. As for writing, I spent years making myself *unhappy* because I wasn't doing it. I thought I'd be happy when I did.

I can't pinpoint the day or hour of the flip but in the last few years I've learned that my own well-being isn't dependent on some **thing** happening (or not happening). I've learned how to stop measuring my inner state of being by the things or people outside of me.

I know, how obvious is that!

So if you have ever said to yourself or someone else "well, you can't buy happiness" or "happiness isn't *out there*," let's get real. We have all said the words without having had the experience of what they really mean at a deeper level.

That experience of un-caused happiness is new, it's totally unfamiliar and life changes almost immediately when you feel it. It is a living force.

That force says to me, "So Elese, we're cool. What would we like to do next?"

It's as if I unhitch the old happiness-if-and-when trailer that was towing all my self-approval and success strategies and just left it on the side of the road.

There is no such condition attached to my writing anymore. There is just writing.

Don't let anyone tell you that when you start feeling good inside you will just want to sit around in some meditative state chanting till you die.

Don't let them tell you that if you can't feel the stress, you won't find the motivation.

Don't let them tell you you'll just feel happy and then life will somehow get boring because you feel so good. It doesn't work like that.

What really happens is without all the noise about what you need to do to be happy, you actually begin to feel good a lot of the time and **from there you see for the first time what's really important to you**. Up until then, it's just guessing, hoping and stabbing in the dark.

Learning what it is like to feel good for no discernable reason is essentially the best thing you can do for yourself.

For me it meant finally getting off my duff, and writing without caring how it turns out.

And if I hadn't decided to write, I guess the downside is I'd simply feel good.

Author's Note
One of my very best shows on this topic is with "Bagger Vance" author, Steven Pressfield, on the psychology of creation (Pressfield, 2011) *and can be heard here:*
http://elesecoit.com/1/post/2011/01/breaking-through-your-blocks-with-steven-pressfield.html

Originally published as Pair #77 on 01/27/2011

To comment or read other comments online go to:
http://www.elesecoit.com/5/post/2011/01/the-difference-between-do-and-dont.html

The Big Why

What's it all for anyway?

Why do we want anything to be different next year? Why do I set the goals I do? Or do the things I do in life or in my work? As I take time off to look ahead (and behind) I'm asking myself what I want and what I'd like to create next year and in particular: why?

- What good is striving to be our absolute best, if excelling gets in the way of your time with your child?
- What good is money if you've lost everything that really matters on the road to getting it?
- Am I doing what is important to me now or am I telling myself to settle for less so I can do what's important someday?
- Is what I'm doing part of making myself into the person I want to wake up with everyday?
- Do I truly need all the things I am so afraid might drop out of my life?

It's likely you know someone who has sacrificed years, skipped holidays, chastised themselves for not being enough, worked all hours to make a big nest egg and then were too ill or tired to do any of the things that they put off to The Great Someday.

What I'm really asking myself is ... for the sake of what?

I am adding this as a sanity check to all my New Year Resolutions.

Originally published as Pair #75 on 12/31/2010

To comment or read other comments online go to:
http://www.elesecoit.com/5/post/2010/12/the-big-why.html

Good, Bad and True Causality

Choice, Change, Challenge and Trial By Fire

It's been a great shock to my system to see that I don't know everything, all of the time.

The huge advances in quantum physics alone should teach us that the real limit to knowledge is our inability to let go of our concepts in order to see something new. A certain amount of inexplicability is bound to be part of life, and may actually be essential to living. Especially if the idea of living is to grow and expand as people and not just to prove that we are right.

You are in for a delicious ride in life If you are willing to doubt the way you see the world and what you've classified as good, bad, right and wrong. If not, life can be very hard on a person.

How deeply we are willing to open to the possibility that things are not as they seem is the measure of how much we can begin to grow. The level to which we are willing to let go into the unknown is the level to which discovery is possible. When discovery finds you — total delight!

This chapter takes a quick glance at our assumptions about choice and our ideas of what is good and bad. To tug at these threads is to have the entire sweater unravel. And this is a comfy old sweater we've all become rather attached to.

There is actually a lot riding on our willingness to pry open our assumptions and have greater neutrality in our ways of seeing. Recovering more quickly and more fully from life's challenges is a direct function our ability to open our eyes and get out of the trees in order to see the forest.

The more we label, the less we connect. The more we blame, the less kindness flows. The world and other people are never going to behave well enough all the time to meet with our approval. All people behave exactly in accordance with the quality of their thinking in any given moment. When we are unable to separate behaviors from the true nature of people, we abandon our own innocence and we cut ourselves off from life's sweetness.

The doorway to connection, intimacy and peace is held open by making room for what we can neither see nor measure – the true inner nature and the invisible essence of people's hearts.

We invite this in whenever we agree to doubt what we see and not-know-it-all. Even just for a moment.

The Good The Bad and The Focus

Don't Look Down!

Things happen every day that we do not like.

Maybe some things are small, like getting a paper cut or breaking a nail. Many things are annoying but no big deal.

Then there are the bigger things: plummeting stocks, an unexpected vet bill, something major goes wrong with your car ... on and on.

We can't rid ourselves of annoyances. Things happen that we cannot control, no matter how much we try to.

If my plane is late or cancelled, I understand that I can't fix or change this as I stand at the ticket desk. But as I stand there who will I be?   I could have any number of experiences, from fury to friendliness, from annoyance to understanding. I can just as well say to myself, "These things happen," as I can say, "This is always happening to me!"

No matter what our so-called personality type we are still choosing our focus.

Focus on certain thoughts will leave us feeling relaxed.

Focus on other thoughts will leave us feeling tense.

We know this is true because we recognize this is the principle at work behind relaxation techniques like petting a cat, or regulated breathing or guided visualization where we might imagine the tension flowing out our feet and into the ground. We change focus. And we shift.

There is so much direct connection between what we think and what we feel, that thinking grateful thoughts and feeling annoyed at the same time is actually impossible.

There are all kinds of random shifts. Perhaps we get in touch with something we appreciate like having great friends (or remembering how lucky I am that I just spent an entire week with my

Dad). We empathize with others, looking around to see those who are having a worse time than we are and perhaps imagining what it's like to be the airline ticket agents who have to be at the sharp end of people's frustrations every day.

To come back to the moment, to calm down, and to let our sanity be restored —whether we use a technique for this purpose or we simply allow the natural way of things to take it's course —will never wipe out stock losses, get planes off the ground or stop time. But we do feel better.

And I'll tell you what else feels better to me: to know that I have choice.

And if I really want to feel bad, I know just how to do that too.

Author's Note
In many situations people find it difficult to change or choose their focus. I know I do. What can help is to notice that your thoughts are always on the move. Something new can occur to you regardless of how tied up you get in a situation. Were this not true, you'd be in the same mood everyday all day long! What you also notice if you pay attention to this movement is that as thought shifts, experience shifts with it. This is actually the principle at work behind any technique. This also explains why techniques sometimes succeed in calming you down and sometimes not.

Originally published as Pair #37 on 05/24/2010

To comment or read other comments online go to:
http://www.elesecoit.com/5/post/2010/05/the-good-the-bad-and-the-focus.html

To Change is Human

Working in the field of transformative change, and talking to people about change everyday, I was reflecting on the nature of change.

Here's a common definition of change: *Change is bad*. **Unless what you need to change is something really bad — then** *Change is good*.

This idea that change, in and of itself, is a negative thing can be easily seen all around us. You'll find it in your own head too ... what is the first thing you say when someone says "I've lost my job"? Is it, "oh, too bad!"

I'm not suggesting that my first response to that should be "oh, how wonderful!" But I do notice that the first response is almost never, "Is that a good thing or a bad thing for you?"

Don't you find that interesting?

That default human setting, "change is bad" just kicked in. And we have other ways of viewing change.

In another of our operating reactions to life, the purpose of change may not in itself be bad, but the purpose of change is to get rid of what is bad (about me, the world, what happens to me). That's very interesting too.

It assumes that we can always know what is good and what is bad, make a clear choice and then kick in the change mechanism.

Now, I'll be the first to say that I am always operating out of what I judge to be good and bad. That's just human. (Not doing the dishes the night before and waking up to a dirty kitchen has got to be bad. Right?) OK, so, totally true in my world. But it doesn't mean that it is in yours.

I'm not suggesting that there is no such thing as bad ever. But I do think it is possible to become more philosophical and to see that we live within a bigger context called life. Not everything that ever happened to us that we judged as bad, turned out to kill us. In fact sometimes, years on it not only didn't kill us, it strengthened us in some way.

Which doesn't mean everything is good no matter what but it does mean that everything contributes to life in some way.

Or, everything is part of life.

Or ... life just is.

Maybe time delivers us a fresh perspective or distance shows us new vantage points or we simply wake up, have a change of heart, or let go. However it happens, change happens.

Isn't that the same thing as saying that things are not always what they seem? Or "There is no good or bad but thinking makes it so?"

Since I'm not content with platitudes, here is what I'm reflecting on: if we could accept the nature of life is change, rather than certainty, wouldn't that make everything easier?

We could remain judging creatures, but begin to consider change natural, normal and perhaps sometimes welcome. It opens up the possibility of not having all the answers all the time — and being OK with that.

I am going to share a story that was sent to me in a longer version. You'll probably recognize it ...

Two Angels.
Two angels are walking the earth in human form and are taken in by a very poor farmer and his wife.

Now when angels come into form, their powers become more limited, and only experienced angels are empowered to intervene in cases of highest need and emergency.

Anyway, when they wake up in the morning the farmer's only cow has died. The farmer and wife are distraught that their only source of milk and some small income has gone forever. Not only that, they've given most of what they had in provisions to their two house guests. They are destitute.

The younger angel, whose miracle powers are strictly limited, says to the elder angel, "How could you let this happen?! They sheltered us for the night and gave us everything even though they had so very little. Surely you should have intervened on their behalf. Now they have nothing!"

He becomes very discouraged and also angry at the cruelty and poor judgment of his companion.

As they set off down the road, the more he ruminates on his mentor angel's terrible decision, the more upset he becomes.

Finally after a long period of walking together the gentle elder says, "Things are not always as they seem little angel," for he had been receiving the silent snarls with kindness and understanding.

"Last night another angel dropped by. It was the angel of Death coming for the wife."

He paused, "I gave him the cow."

Author's Note
Check out my radio show, Get Off Your Own Back
http://www.elesecoit.com/1/post/2011/04/get-off-your-own-back.html

Originally published as Pair #86 on 04/07/2011

To comment or read other comments online go to:
http://www.elesecoit.com/5/post/2011/04/waking-up-to-the-dead-cow.html

*Life is hard and then you get your a*s handed to you*

Ever thought ...

"It's been years now, but I just can't forgive so and so."
"Every time I hear his voice, I just want to slump on the floor and cry."
"I can't stop thinking about how much they hurt me and it makes me so mad."
"I've just been told they are not sure if it's treatable. My life is over."

No one disputes that you have good reasons to feel bad when you've just been told you have a disease or that your job is gone. And **I'm not saying you should feel great and wonderful on the heels of some difficult life moment. Yet I am interested in how we explain our feelings about them.** Because where we look for the cause of our feelings has everything to do with our recovery.

Although anger, grief, self-admonition, regret and concern are normal responses, we are often looking to resolve these emotions in the completely the wrong place. For years I remember thinking that if my father apologized to me for a particular event then finally I could feel better, put the grievance behind me and get on with life. Because of this kind of thinking I wallowed in my own bad feelings for years without any resolution, understanding or forward movement. Despite therapy, counseling and body work.

I knew I was stuck in the past. I think we've all experienced this and the helplessness that goes with it.

It seems like all the pain is coming from outside of us. It certainly seemed that way to me!

So let's consider for a moment how it is any *outside* experiences get *inside* of us.

How did my father, who lived far away, actually make me miserable over the years via an event that was long over and done with? How is it, for example that cancer actually creates emotional disturbance? How is that someone else uses their power to create sadness in you? How does that process, that alleged transference, actually work?

If you examine closely you will see that it doesn't. All of my pain was old history carried through time — by me. The same is true of everything we feel pain about, trivial or serious.

Consider this as an example. Let's take a friend of mine who knows someone at work who is very "negative."   My friend will tell you that this person has such bad energy they can get into his space (or anyone else's) and ruin his day.

Know anyone right now who has that power in your world?

My friend told me, "There are just some people who have bad energy, and when they are around they are going to affect you. That's just not something you can change."

I considered that for a moment. How does that work?

I asked him, "Is there ever a time when that person doesn't affect you that way?"

"Well, sometimes. When I'm in a good mood after the weekend. I just go, 'Whatever, dude!'"

"And are there some people who are friends with him," I responded, "and who don't seem to think he has this 'bad energy?'"

"Well, yeah, actually. Which is strange."

"It is strange isn't it? How is that possible do you think?" I wondered with him. "If he is the cause of the 'bad vibe', you would think he'd always be — not only for you but for everyone."

Why this difference? Is it the behavior of the person or is it the attitude of the observer?

Someone I know discovered this for herself recently she noticed how her own annoyance with a colleague would rise up in her. As she puts it, "All I have to do is hear her shoes coming down the hall!"

As if the shoes created the feelings.

What we know about life but often forget, is that no person or thing really has the power to make us feel anything at all. We are sovereign in our feelings.

What we do is look around and ATTRIBUTE our feelings.

But that doesn't give the shoes power.

Looking outside for the causes of our inside feelings is a mis-attribution of cause.

Feelings don't arise out of nowhere. They are not provoked out of us by job losses or diagnosis. They arise from the thoughts, judgments and stories we create about life around us and about what things mean.

So it is actually very true to say that things are not always what they seem because we are not really seeing. We are perceiving and experiencing via our thoughts. Like the projector shows whatever film is on. **You feel what's happening in you. Not what is out there.**

And that is good news on many fronts.

It means that you have the ability to have new ways of seeing things occur to you. You have the capacity that your heart may open suddenly without notice. The capacity to feel good is lying there within you and can pop to the surface anytime like a cork bobbing in the water. There is no limit and no barrier on your capacity for joy, love, and wisdom. Because you never learned those things, they just came with your human firmware installation.

And because of that, you really can relax.

So whenever a good feeling comes up naturally for you, you might like to notice: that just happens.

When I began to relax and see that all my past was gone and that my feelings were coming from my own thoughts, my father and I became the great friends that I always hoped we would be.

What I've noticed is that I have a natural tendency toward upwards. Toward love. Toward reconciliation. It is beautiful that we actually tend naturally toward good feeling. We can miss that wonderful fact when we are pointing the finger away from ourselves.

Originally published as Pair #95 on 06/17/2011

To comment or read other comments online go to:
http://www.elesecoit.com/5/post/2011/06/what-to-do-when-you-are-bitch-slapped-by-life.html

---

The Fluffy Stuff

Show me the evidence!

You know there is a difference between *Hard Skills* and *Soft Skills* when you tell your parents you are leaving medical school to study sociology.

Hard skills are things like adding numbers and hammering nails. It's the stuff we consider employable and usable.

Soft skills are things like relating and intuition. Which we consider nice but optional.

In business, soft skills are the first training expenditures to be dropped when budget restrictions hit; it's harder to understand the ROI (Return On Investment) on communication skills, than it is for bookkeeping.

How much we undervalue the softer skills of life came home to me as I heard Kevin Laye[21] demonstrate Thought Field Therapy. TFT is a quick and effective way of ending stress, phobias and a host of other modern complaints. Kevin uses TFT to resolve physical pain in people within minutes and he gave many examples of the absolute effectiveness of his work.

In the discussion with Kevin, he was asked about the hard science behind why this works.

Kevin's response got me to thinking. He asked the audience to consider that there are things we know exist but can't prove with measurable science. Yet they work regardless. He put it roughly this way:

Think of someone you love. Everyone has someone or an animal they love.

He asked the group to consider how they would measure that love.

In inches?
Centimeters?
Miles?
Where does that love live? Your brain? Your physical heart? Your blood?

How would you show it to me or take it from place to place - In a box? A wheelbarrow? In a thimble?

Love is something we know exists. Yet we cannot prove it exists with physical evidence.

I don't think he was suggesting TFT works because of love but rather pointing out that **many things that we accept exist and know are real, we neither can see nor measure.**

If you look around don't you ever wonder what that certain something is that successful people have? Don't we say, "I wish I could bottle that?" We are talking about something beyond technical competence. Yet when we make our own choices, we will very often choose to acquire more competencies and hard skills.

It just got me to thinking how many things that are essential to a good life are the softer skills — immeasurable and formless and yet immeasurably valuable. I thought how often I'd made learning decisions based on what seemed practical and ignored the fluffy stuff because I was unsure of the ROI. That cost me in the long run.

Every time we hesitate to invest in growing and developing our entire selves, and not just our "hard" skills, we forget this.

Or maybe we just don't believe that a good life is possible, only a technically competent one.

Originally published as Pair #31 on 05/13/2010

To comment or read other comments online go to:
http://www.elesecoit.com/5/post/2010/05/the-fluffy-stuff.html

Gratitude

When You Are Down and Troubled, Wishing on Stars and Still Breathing

Here is one of the single most interesting things about Gratitude: no one ever taught you how to do it.

Gratitude is one of those things you just already know. You didn't intellectually learn it. No one sat you down and gave you lessons. You can't hold it in your hand. You can't deliver it in a bag. You can't measure it. But you know that you can feel it and you know the unmistakable feeling of it.

When gratitude it is there you recognize it and it recognizes you. It is, very simply, an innate part of you. You learned it like you learned breathing.

Here is another thing about Gratitude. Everyone has it. No exceptions.

Just like a new computer comes pre-loaded with an operating system, you came pre-loaded with capacities for love, deep feeling, gratitude, joy, compassion and much more. These constitute a human before and beyond the body. They constitute you and I. This formless operating system, or essence, existed before we arrived and will exist after we are gone.

When you are feeling gratitude you are partaking in universal humanhood and universal divinehood. You are experiencing the oneness of all of us in essence. In our capacity to feel grateful and to have an experience of what is formless, no one is left out. We are all the same.

Here is another thing about Gratitude in particular. It just arises. Isn't that amazing?

It floats up in the moment. It is always available and always buoyant. When you turn to find it, it is waiting for you. It is an ever-present response to a prayer in the now. A grace. It is there.

Notice how this grace simply gets hold of you. Notice how it is there whenever you are not thinking about how difficult your problems are and how your life sucks.

Look up and you will see it everywhere. And it is everywhere you go because you are.

That's quite a lot to be grateful for.

Wish on Your Own Star

I made a wish for all the newly graduated Transformative Coaches from Michael Neill's Supercoach Academy[3]

May the urge to know yourself
and express all that you are
be too strong for you to resist

I wish this for us all.

Originally published as Pair #52 on 06/16/2010

To comment or read other comments online go to:
http://www.elesecoit.com/5/post/2010/06/making-a-wish.html

Still Breathing After All These Years

Dear Diary, A good day today. Woke up.

Over lunch my Mom and I reminisced about how when I was growing up we decided not to celebrate birthdays. Instead my brother and I were accorded a "special day" we could chose to be anytime of the year on any particular day.

I was particularly in favor of this idea because my birthday falling in July meant I never got cards or a cake at school like other kids with birthdays during the school year. While I was picturing school parties and lots of presents, the real reason for our family choice was that my mother and father raised us in Christian Science.[22] When your fundamental operating principle is that our true identity is spirit and the physical world is not real, but an illusion, it follows that it might not make much sense to celebrate the passage of time.

Most of my life I spent questioning this and other ideas I was raised with but I have to admit, we had something when it came to the birthday thing.

Cakes, presents and all the rest are fun but perhaps the point of today is really to be happy to be here. Period. When you consider that the past is gone and the future does not exist, then each moment is a kind of lucky break. It's a new now in the grace of simply being alive.

That is something to remember everyday. Glad to be here. Glad to be alive.

Breathe.

Originally published as Pair #61 on 07/27/2010

To comment or read other comments online go to:
http://www.elesecoit.com/5/post/2010/07/still-breathing-after-all-these-years.html

"When you're down and troubled ..."

Phone a Friend

**"*When you're down and troubled*
and you need some loving care
and nothing, oh, nothing is going right..."**
(James Taylor and Carol King, "You've Got A Friend")

I was thinking back over some of the really hard times in my life, times when I was dumped, stalked or just plain broke, when I realized something really huge. I realized that everything I was so convinced that I wouldn't survive — *I had.*

I am here. But the really BIG thing that occurred to me was the way I had got through most of those times was thanks to friends.

There were friends who gave me places to stay, friends who took me out to cheer me up, friends who listened and friends who told me the truth when I didn't want to hear it.

In short there were people, throughout my life and at key moments, who simply wouldn't allow me to fall all the way.

To all those wonderful people: thank you. I am eternally grateful.

If God exists, I am thinking that maybe he shows up in the form of your friends.

Originally published as Pair #32 on 05/16/2010

To comment or read other comments online go to:
http://elesecoit.com/5/post/2010/05/when-youre-down-and-troubled.html

Happiness

Watching Our Language, Welcoming The Bad and Getting a Life

When we think of what happiness is and what it is not, it's easy to get it all wrong.

It is perhaps one of our most misunderstood words. For something we spend a great deal of time pursuing, we sure seem to spend relatively little time quietly reflecting on. So our ideas of happiness remain just that, "ideas about happiness" rather than experiences of being happy.

We have more assumptions about happiness than just about anything else. We are more disappointed by our own predictions of what will make us happy than just about anything else. We don't necessarily even get better at these predictions over time! There is nothing we want more, and nothing we've looked for in more wrong places.

No wonder people give up on the whole idea of happiness and settle for a regular income or steady relationship instead! Happiness is illusive, slippery and evasive and seems always to be just around the corner. You can hardly blame yourself for giving up on happiness – as a notion, that is.

But happiness, if you think about it, is neither a thing nor a notion. It is not a destination or a stop along the way. Happiness is not a luxury or a "good idea."

We keep trying to create happiness as a by-product of some form of goodness, a good life, being a good person. But happiness happens to good and bad people and to people in good and bad situations. There is no deserving involved.

At times I see an intimate connection between happiness and truth, but can't explain this. When I see the truth, happiness appears to be there as well. Perhaps that's getting lined up with Life. Or maybe glimpsing that Life is a neutral canvas to which I bring the colored paint.

I know that despite all my predictions, I have made it through and survived all my unhappy moments. I know that although I thought unhappiness was to be avoided and happiness was to be sought, it turns out I really could have just relaxed. Unhappy feelings could not hurt me.

I didn't understand that for some time. In my concern I failed to notice that happiness has ever been my constant companion, an arm round my shoulder, walking patiently with me all along.

Weather forecast: a bad day ahead

I was observing the fog over the ocean the other day. In a matter of minutes the fog rolled in and the huge expanse of ocean simply blended away. Gone.

It was as if there was no more ocean. Just grey all around.

You know the saying that *just because the clouds are there doesn't mean the sun has gone?* We use that to try to buck ourselves up when things get hard. It's a way of saying we should have faith because the sun will come back. But really, why do we need faith? Faith is hard. Faith is a struggle. Faith asks me to believe what I don't believe and still be comfortable and happy.

But beyond that, why do I need to know the sun is going to come back anyway?

Reflecting on the scene in front of me I thought, not only is the ocean not gone but the ocean is also entirely unaware of my perceptions and opinions of it. It really doesn't give a monkey's if it is hidden or in plain site. Just as the sun doesn't care if the clouds roll over it. And the sky doesn't care about whether it is experiencing a hurricane. It is entirely neutral.

Life is entirely neutral.

I, on the other hand, am not.

Ever watched a nature program and felt sadness or horror when the lion tumbles and kills the pretty gazelle?

We add all the opinions to what we see.

The weather is a useful example of how we do this all day long. When we have casual conversations about forecasts we are not talking about the weather, but about our opinions of the weather. "It's going to rain AGAIN today," "it's going to stay nice ALL day," and "it's going to be 20 degrees today!" are not facts, they are predictors of the day I'm about to have.

And I make them.

Human life is so interesting, isn't it? It's natural to have opinions about things. At the same time, there's that ocean. Just being there.

I'm certainly not experiencing the neutrality of life all day long. But I am glad to know that my own state of mind is ultimately is responsible for the quality of my life experience.

I find that infinitely more encouraging than a life being blown by about by the four winds.

Author's Note
I recommend listening to Jack Pransky[23] and I talk about the nature of life experience on the show: "Simple Truths for Living Well"
http://www.elesecoit.com/1/post/2010/10/simple-truths-for-living-well.html

Originally published as Pair #94 on 06/15/2011

To comment or read other comments online go to:
http://www.elesecoit.com/5/post/2011/06/get-a-life.html

6 Word Swaps That Will Save Your Life

The Less-Than Cunning Linguist

1. Convert the word "maybe" to a clear "yes" or "no."
2. Swap the words "I think …" to "In my experience what I notice is …"
3. Change your next complaint into a clear request.
4. Use the words "I will" only for real promises you intend to keep.
5. Shut up (and listen instead of saying anything*).
6. Say "tell me more" instead of giving an opinion.

Will you let me know what happens when you try these out?

They really have changed my life.

Originally published as Pair #24 on 05/03/2010

To comment or read other comments online go to:
http://www.elesecoit.com/5/post/2010/05/6-word-swaps-that-will-change-your-life.html

Welcome The Bad

Here comes Mr. Brightside

Don't you just hate it when you are in the middle of something painful and someone says, "Well you have to look on the bright side!"?

Not that I'm against positive thinking but I don't think it really cheers anyone up to pretend they feel fine when they don't. You know how it feels to have someone being all smiles and telling you they are not mad while they are clenching their teeth and fists? It's downright scary.

The only way it works for me to look on the bright side is if the bright side is true.

I've never been able to fake myself into happiness.

I have found, however, that happiness is not ever far away even in the worst of times.

Here's my theory. Think of anything bad that's happened to you, maybe losing a job or breaking up with someone you thought would always be in your life. In my experience, as the years passed, I managed to appreciate the opportunities that these moments of loss created: I found new love and a job I love, for example.

What that means is, with time, I've always been able to enjoy some benefit. So why not just compress time? I'll either get the lesson now, or I can have it later. I might as well just shake hands, get acquainted and spare myself the wait.

Maybe that is really the only choice we are ever making.

Originally published as Pair #59 on 07/21/2010

To comment or read other comments online go to:
http://www.elesecoit.com/5/post/2010/07/welcome-the-bad.html

Anyone seen my happiness lying around?

When I attended Robert Holden's Coaching Happiness training[24] I really experienced the power of asking myself deep questions about happiness ... and then listening for the answers.

What Robert brought home to me was the power of asking questions like, "What is Happiness for me?"

He treated Happiness, not as a destination, but as an inquiry.

Here are some of my fave quotes from Robert that week

"When we forget who we are, we forget what happiness is"

"Happiness is a non-deserving issue"

"Happiness is the experience of your true nature"

"Will your choices help you be happy Now ... or Eventually?"

Where am I with my own inquiry into happiness? Funny you should ask.

For me, today, happiness is relaxing into me exactly as I am and exactly as I am not.

Self-love and self-acceptance may sound pretty dumb when rolled up into pat utterances like "love yourself" or "I'm OK, You're OK" but when you reflect on what looks like, it can become meaningful.

What is happiness?

It is, when ...

I stop trying to become.

I'm kind and loving.

I'm not believing all my small thoughts about myself.

I'm not trying to rid myself of anything.
.
Happiness is when I look and really see that I'm always just one thought away from happiness.

How encouraging.

Author's Note
To hear my radio shows with Robert Holden exploring the keys to happiness go to:

http://elesecoit.com/1/post/2009/06/the-ten-keys-to-happiness-with-robert-holden.html

http://elesecoit.com/1/post/2009/07/the-ten-and-then-some-keys-to-happiness-part-ii-with-robert-holden.html

Originally published as Pair #67 on 09/02/2010

To comment or read other comments online go to:
http://www.elesecoit.com/5/post/2010/09/what-is-happiness.html

Inspiration, Insight and Creativity

Messages From The Wrong Side of The Bed and The Feel of Clarity

We have romantic notions about inspiration: It flashes. It deserts us. It's inborn talent. It's a gift. We think it lands on our shoulders or whispers in our ear. These ways of talking about our inspired moments may also lead us astray. They make creativity into something mythical and selective. They put us in charge of preparing the landing strip for the muse's arrival.

It is easy to think there are preconditions to our creative processes: from having a positive attitude, to clearing out the cupboards, to having an advanced degree – even that we must be someone else! These notions are precisely what get us all wound up and worried, making creativity inaccessible. I hunker down, convinced I must act quickly and do more. What if inspiration deserts me? As I tinker and toil, sweat, tweak and strain, the further away it seems.

What have I forgotten? I've missed the one truth thing about the nature of creativity: a new idea is always possible. Insights do not come in finite numbers. As far as I know there are no real restrictions on the conditions for arrival and no rationing to the worthy.

If you have ever cleared a garden or trimmed a bush you'll know that it doesn't take long before brand new sprouts arrive. Tiny green urgings push quickly through the new cement you've poured and the terrain you've so carefully weeded. Unstoppably. Endlessly.

We forget that we humans too are part of Life longing to express itself. We can't stop that. And we can't force it. We are simply not in charge of it and yet we are intimately and inextricably part of that constant surge. Understand this and you are back to sweet clarity.

If you think you can be unplugged from life itself, think again. Within each of us it blooms in the form of our own special petals. Where it comes from is both within us and beyond us. When you cut yourself, your skin begins the healing process immediately. So too, your access to new insight and fresh ideas is unfettered and requires no force from you to be accomplished.

Another way to think of it is buoyancy. While we may all bathe in worry or stressful thinking sometimes, we can never stop the upward push of ideas. It is their nature to pop to the surface like a float. That's what they do.

We don't need to control that, nor be concerned about it, because we can count on it.

No positive attitude required

How can you not fall in love with someone who tells you that you can write your book, get your message out and do whatever it is you came here to do, even if you wake up on the wrong side of the bed every day for the rest of your life?

Barbara Sher's[25] Absolute Guaranteed Secret to Success

You do not need to believe in yourself...
http://youtu.be/mlHgW3VihME

Originally published as Pair #74 on 11/19/2010

To comment or read other comments online go to:
http://www.elesecoit.com/5/post/2010/11/messages-that-matter.html

Pick up a pen and listen

I wrote a letter to God.

I did. I sat down and wrote "Dear God," and then I kept going.

Funnily enough, it was incredibly soothing. I was writing and as I did, I was just working out on paper some of my concerns and worries. As I continued *writing out loud*, things started to change, answers started to come to me and some insights flowed out on to the page.

It's interesting how writing longhand can take you just enough outside yourself.

It does a couple of other amazing things too.

It slows you down. And when you slow down you start to get much clearer about the nature of the problem.

I could clearly hear all the thoughts that are running around up there in my head, agitated and afraid, and how seriously I was taking them.

Once something is down on paper in your lap there is just no ignoring the ridiculousness of some of what you think: "so-and-so needs to do this" or "this damn well better change" or "God, you are going to have to take over on this one!"

A teeny tyrant that wants to run the world is talking and talking and talking and has so much to say ... not much of it helpful.

How the heck are we supposed to have good ideas, be creative or do any kind of planning or problem solving with that mess going on?

If you keep up the flow long enough and ignore the desire to stop and wallow or actually take the words seriously, something funny can happen.

Calm descends and things settle down.

And then some wise or bright solution may drop in.

Or a light comes on.

And that's wonderful.

Now I'm not saying God descends with an answer. In fact I have every reason from my own life to believe it does not work that way.

But wisdom does come. It comes from inside or from wherever it feels like it comes from: the field, the present, the moment, the calmness, your brain. It doesn't matter. The fact is that it comes.

And it creeps up on you and blooms wherever you have enough space for it. Like a blade of grass through concrete.

I realize it wouldn't matter who I address the letter to, it would have the same effect.

And funnily enough, I can see now that writing "Dear God" is just another way of writing to myself.

Author's Note
Mandy Evan's talks to me about the nature of life, miracles and infinite opportunity:
http://www.elesecoit.com/1/post/2010/09/break-out-to-miracles.html

Originally published as Pair #79 on 02/10/2011

To comment or read other comments online go to:
http://www.elesecoit.com/5/post/2011/02/the-most-ridiculous-thing-ive-done-in-a-long-time.html

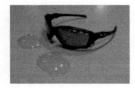

When The Scales Fall

Much I as would rather hear positive thinking than negative, I'll take my own feeble insights over inspirational sips from someone else's fountain any day.

Maybe I should explain myself, for I realize that "insight" could be defined in many ways.

I'm going to define insight as what happens in us when we have a moment of realization about the truth of our world and our experience.

Perhaps we notice what works and what doesn't for us. Perhaps we notice the link between things. Perhaps we have an AHA! of some sort based on seeing something a new way, even when we've encountered it many times before.

Insights are personal, specific to us and don't always (or maybe even ever) apply to other people. Although when shared they can have value for others, the main value of an insight is that it tends to reset the direction of our own inner compass.

And it happens in a wisp of a moment.

Sometimes for me that feels like the moment I take a stand. Other times I feel that sense of release. Other times it is a feeling of recognition of when wisdom is in the room and when it is not which I call, "this, not that."

But it is always sweet clarity.

No matter whether we are talking to a friend or a coach, the moments that have the most meaning are those when our own insights pop up in plain view. Like a balloon we've tried to hold underwater.

That's why advice from others is so unnecessary ...

... and more often than not, unwelcome.

The biggest disservice we can render anyone is to try to replace their wisdom with our own.

Originally published as Pair #43 on 06/01/2010

To comment or read other comments online go to:
http://www.elesecoit.com/5/post/2011/02/the-most-ridiculous-thing-ive-done-in-a-long-time.html

Inspiration vs. Perspiration (and what I learned from Michael Neill)

If it's not art, what is it?

I spent a year as an apprentice to Michael Neill[8] and I can tell you there is one thing Michael knows better than anyone and that's how to **tip the balance of life toward inspiration**.

When you consider that many of us struggle to get out of perspiration and into inspiration even for a short minute it's a source of hope to watch Michael proving there's another way.

The quirky thing about Michael's brand of inspired is that he works very hard: in an effortless kind of way. Now, I don't propose that Michael's or anyone's life as the "THE formula" but it's certainly worth thinking about this.

The idea of "Living an Inspired Life" sounds magical, spiritual, artsy and deeply cool — and like a land far, far, away.

Real inspiration, funnily enough, is so mundane and everyday that we miss it. Rather than the big bang smacking you in the face to reveal your life purpose and the secrets of the universe, it might be more like being amazed that you just opened your eyes … "I woke up today! What next?"

And here's the thing about people who are genuinely in touch with the miracle it is to wake up again so they can do the things they enjoy: very often they also just happen to be successful.

Or maybe put another way, successful people seem to also love what they do.

So which comes first?

How many are hoping the success is what will bring the satisfaction?

How many won't be satisfied until they have the success?

I think living inspired is a minor art. And "Inspired" is a terrible word for it really.   It is just not the get-psyched-up and go-getter thing. Nor does it mean I put a flower behind my right ear and dedicate my life to verse. From what I can tell it is the simple art of genuinely falling in love with life.

Then, of course, when you are in love with your life, hard work can be a big part of it.

Sometimes you toil hard and you sweat.

Other times you rest and float.

Maybe it is not so much a balance between % inspiration and % perspiration, as it is letting inspiration decide what's worth sweating over while you've got that smile on your face.

Originally published as Pair #25 on 05/04/2010

To comment or read other comments online go to:
http://elesecoit.com/5/post/2010/05/inspiration-vs-perspiration-and-what-i-learned-from-michael-neill.html

---

Love

We would be so much better off if we made love a life-long query rather than a lifetime quest.

Most of what we do to find love is in itself a barrier to love. We measure what we give and what comes back and watch vigilantly over this balance sheet. We punish certain behaviors, and demand conformity with our ideals. Most of all, we want everyone else to go first.

If you take a moment to consider the relationships you know of or the ones you have in your life, would you describe most of the behaviors you observe as loving or fearful? Getting or Giving? Controlling or Free? Intimate or Guarded? How much love do you see around you? How much are you giving? Have you ever been offered unconditional love and let it in?

When it comes to love, we have mostly getting behaviors. See if you recognize your flavor:

Trying to elicit more lovable behaviors from others before you will give your love.
Trying to coax others into loving you by making your own behaviors more lovable.

We stay at the shallow end of the pool when it comes to love and yet we think we are out there swimming with the sharks. We try to perfect the conditions for love's appearance, rather than looking more deeply into others and ourselves for the source of Love itself.

How do we recognize love? Is it the overwhelming feeling of desire? It is the sentimental feeling of missing someone? Is it the devastating feeling of losing someone?

If you truly, truly, want a happy life start by stripping out the old wallpaper of your dried up, peeling, moldy imaginings about love. In this chapter I bust a few of my own false concepts and share some of the realizations that have literally turned my world inside out.

When I looked underneath it all, I noticed Love never seemed to have a goal or an agenda. Love never wanted anything from another person. I did. But Love didn't. Love itself had no conditions attached. Love loved me no matter what I was doing. When I lifted my pre-conceptions and laid down my bargaining chips, love was my knee-jerk reaction to everything.

You too may find that Love has no purpose, but that the purpose of all relationships is Love.

What's love got to do with it?

I know now that there are many things I did not understand about love. I never thought I needed to ask or find out. I thought I knew.

I never asked, for example, what is love really made of?

What does it look like for me?

I assumed I would know it when I saw it. Or worse, perhaps, I just accepted without thinking about it at all and assumed it looked like the images in romantic movies or wedding photographs.

Without much inquiry it's easy to think that love consists entirely of a feeling and that feeling is elation, excitement, heat, etc.

From whatever angle you look, it is very easy to see love as something that is out there to get or find ... or lose.

If someone we like the look of arrives and gives us attention, we think, "It's here!" If someone approves of us — it's here! We feel great. We feel loved. And then it's gone.

We begin to keep an eye open, looking for it to pop up again like a happy accident in our lives.

When we get fed up waiting, we try to induce it. A lot of celebrity behavior screams, "Please love me!" Don't you think we are all a bit like that? Love-getters. Self-improvement too, is an attempt to love ourselves without ever asking the question "What does that mean?"

As I've opened up more questions like those above, I have come to recognize love as an experience of goodwill and connectedness with others and myself. It has a lot of flavors, ranging from deep gratitude, to acceptance and compassion for someone's pain, to the warmest feeling of wanting the best for someone.

I may not experience all of the flavors all the time but real Love is totally unlike romantic gushy-love.

Here is one more thing about love that was a new discovery for me: Love is instantly available to me all the time.

Now that would be impossible given the way I used to think.

It may still seem like love is something that comes and goes based on what someone is doing – being nice or being mean. But when I've been open to challenging ideas about love and made a practice to love others on a deeper level, no matter what is happening and no matter what they are doing, I find that love is there.

It's available. I don't have to look for it or wait for it.

If you also know that is really true, it means it is possible to love everyone and yourself all the time.

That makes love a choice, not a response.

Author's Note
In this radio show I reflect on learning unconditional loving kindness:
http://www.elesecoit.com/1/post/2010/11/the-greatest-thing-youll-ever-learn.html

Originally published as Pair #60 on 07/26/2010

To comment or read other comments online go to:
http://www.elesecoit.com/5/post/2010/07/be-nice-so-i-can-love-you.html

Let The Games Begin!

Talking to my Dad on the phone a while ago and I remember he said, "I understand now that every time we meet someone, no matter whom, the purpose is always love."

I pulled over to the side of the road to consider this for a moment.

He went on:

"I've realized the problem of my life is that I would meet someone and immediately think I knew or could quickly figure out what kind of love, exactly.

Then I would try to force everything and them into that mold.

What a disaster.

Now I know just to love and allow things to unfold to where they naturally settle and be whatever they are supposed to be."

Could I, too, I wondered, just open up to the idea that I might not know what any single encounter might be for?

Do I really need to know the purpose of every relationship from the moment we meet?

What sense does it make for me to size people up against a list or quickly make up my mind what role they'll play in my life?

Does that really make my relationships easy, open, friendly and fun?

Or does it immediately turn them into scoreboards with rule sets and referees?

And sometimes we haven't even agreed what game we are both playing!

Don't you hate it when your Dad's right?

Author's Note
My Dad writes about his experiences learning to listen to and follow his inner voice. Go figure. His books are available here: http://www.amazon.com/Lee-Coit/e/B000APH0WG.

You can hear my father and I on the radio show: http://elesecoit.com/1/post/2010/12/living-above-the-chaos-with-lee-coit.html

There is also a tremendous show with August Turak[26] in which we explore purpose, meaning, and how it is in our interest to forget our self-interest. http://www.elesecoit.com/1/post/2010/03/the-alchemy-of-transformation-or-scrooge-and-the-purpose-of-life.html

---

Originally published as Pair #29 on 05/10/2010

To comment or read other comments online go to:
http://elesecoit.com/5/post/2010/05/father-knows-best.html

Truth Serums

You can say anything to anyone when you do two things:

- Love them unconditionally
- Take everything you are about to say and apply it to yourself first

Before you are about to speak a great Truth to someone, try it.

Let me know if that doesn't work.

Originally published as Pair #44 on 06/02/2010

To comment or read other comments online go to:
http://www.elesecoit.com/5/post/2010/06/how-to-say-anything-to-anyone.html

Mystery, Curiosity and Wonderment

Losing Our Religion, Lots Can Happen, The Great Unknown and Other Curios

When did we decide that to know is better than to not-know?

The desire to know, or worse, the desire to look like we know is a modern plague. In a fell swoop it destroys listening, understanding, cooperation and learning. It undermines peace of mind and peace amongst nations.

Consumed by our desire to know or not admit that we don't, we finish other people's sentences, we hate people we have never met and we cling to things we have long outgrown.

Living in the world of familiarity means our lives are choked off by the smallness of our own ideas. Crowded in by the known we become selectors instead of creators. The death of curiosity was surely the birth of the ego, as children give up on being explorers of wild imaginings and doodads without names and become regurgitators of facts from 10-year old textbooks.

Our lack of curiosity leads directly to our unwillingness to fail and spreads from there to our unwillingness to try – because we already know. We know too much. And what we know isn't worth learning.

To allow wonder and mystery into your life is to suddenly find yourself in weightless spaciousness. We work so hard to fuel personal creativity, business and product innovation, but we would automatically have all of these if we added just an extra dash of curiosity to our daily vitamin supplements.

Imagine not knowing your boss, not knowing your children, not knowing yourself – being totally open. You'd listen closely. You would see new and amazing things. You'd discover the people you live with are people you've never met before. In the freshness of the moment you would unable to locate that familiar feeling of disconnection.

You would see into how your world is constructed. You would gasp to realize you are much bigger than you ever imagined.

You would lose your fear.

It's a Curious Thing...

No wonder

Hey, what's happened to curiosity?

Did it do something wrong?

Did it get relegated to the third division?

When did we decide that all things have answers and that life is a search for definitive solutions and no questions should be left undone? We turned life into the multiple choice quiz and removed the option "None of the above."

I was thinking this week and I wrote down on my pad next to me:

"What if all life were the adventure of finding out, rather than finding?"

Maybe it is the nature of the human mind that has become so petrified by the discomfort of not knowing that it will settle for a poor answer or a half-truth before it admits it does not know.

Or has it just become **not cool to not know?**

I thought there used to be joy in the process of discovery. Didn't we use to like a bit of mystery?

The word "wonder" is to ponder and consider. It's open. It shrugs its shoulders a bit. It has patience. Christmas used to be a holiday of wonder, right?

We have Seven Wonders in this World.

Actually, only 7?

That's not a lot of Wonder.

Apparently, to be unsure is to be invisible. The humiliation of the admitting you have no answer is actually worse than hoofing something indefensible or silly. Ever seen someone defend a totally made-up statement because they got cornered by their own uncertainty?

Remember in 1985 Ronald Reagan asserted that there was no word in Russian for "Freedom." (It is SVOBODA).

Last time you were lost in a car did you hear: "Actually, dear, no, I'm not sure which road to take or where we are."

Well, we can all recognize ourselves here. I certainly see myself.

Having said that, I can't tell you the weight that lifts when I say, "I'm not sure."

Try it on for size

"I don't know. But I wonder... "

What do you think?

Author's Note
You may wish to check out my radio show on Living in The Unknown
http://www.elesecoit.com/1/post/2012/01/welcoming-the-unknown.html

Originally published as Pair #71 on 09/16/2010

To comment or read other comments online go to:
http://www.elesecoit.com/5/post/2010/09/its-a-curious-thing.html

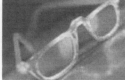

It's all a mystery to me. Thank goodness.

It's interesting to me that something like 80- 90% percent of people in the world declare a religious affiliation. Of that number, the huge majority of people have actually remained with the faith they grew up in and that is, overwhelmingly, the faith of their parents' parents.

This says a lot about our movement from childhood to adulthood, doesn't it?

While it is probably true that many of us don't actually attend church nowadays, I do see that when the going gets rough and when people do look in the direction of a spiritual solution, their start point is often a return to the faith of childhood.

I'm not saying this is a bad thing. Far from it. People I know who've gone back to church when becoming sick or desperate often find comfort and help. In my personal view, any interest in the spiritual nature of life and any inquiry into the nature of who we are, why we are the way we are and how we work as humans, brings us back to something that we are often missing in our modern lives.

Mystery.

We have an odd relationship with mystery these days. Although we are content with fantasy video games and elaborate 3D mega-productions (and we are mildly uncomfortable with serendipitous-ness) we are wildly unfamiliar with the territory of true mystery.

Yet, **despite our will to scientifically know and dissect matter itself, we keep uncovering more mystery.**

Black holes are a mystery.

Why some people overcome cancer and others do not is a mystery.

Where the will to live comes from is a mystery.

Although mystery is quite delicious, I sense that mystery is a bit on the outs these days. And because we've collectively agreed that life can be known, that it can be broken down to the smallest element and contained, we are rarely amazed by life.

Since we are not all that friendly with the inexplicable, we are also rarely reflective. And that IS a shame.

Deep reflection is something almost no one I know engages in regularly. The reason, I suspect? No time. We are all too busy being busy. Even busy waiting for the vacation in order to stop and relax.

But I'm not talking about resting up. I'm talking about reflecting on our lives. I'm talking about hearing the inside of us. Receiving a truly new idea. **Take all the classes on authenticity that you want, you'll never be authentically you until you are reflecting on your intimate life and listening for the answers within you.**

As we have grown to adulthood and left behind our childish things, we may or may not have left behind our churches but we have coupled up with the science of knowing and in doing so have let go of our love of mystery.

At the same time, maybe religions have attempted to explain too much, replacing true mystery and direct knowing with belief. Belief demands that we chose. Mystery does not. Mystery asks that we simply be with.

Surely adulthood does not mean finding more and more answers, but rather being more comfortable with not knowing what the hell is going on.

Originally published as Pair #98 on 06/28/2011

To comment or read other comments online go to:
http://elesecoit.com/5/post/2011/06/losing-our-religion.html

Lots Can Happen

Here's to not knowing

One of the things I've learned about myself and also about my business over the years is: "Lots can happen."

Lots can happen. Make that a motto.

I don't have to look far in my life to see the truth in this.

Sometimes things shift in the very moment I'm thinking, "This will never happen!"

And the only times I've really regretted are the times I wasted worrying something would never happen that I didn't have control over anyway.

Then there all the things I missed because I was looking the other way.

What if we:

- Don't assume today is a predictor of anything at all
- Don't assume today's "No" or today's numbers mean anything about tomorrow
- Assume we don't know
- Assume what we see cannot possibly be ALL there is

To live in a world where we don't assume does not mean we are taking in zero information. But it does mean evaluating information differently.

Like refusing to make everything mean something about me!

I want to strip away all the meaning that we make about how things WILL turn out, all our predictive and unfounded scenarios (all attitudes that shut down our creativity) and focus on what I do not know.

Out of what I do not know comes all possibility.

Please pull out your project plans now and look them over and ask yourself:

Where have I left room for what I do not yet know?

Where have I shut myself down because I am assuming I know everything and what everything means?

Where have I made mistakes because I am assuming that the limits of my thinking are equal to the limits of my possibilities?

Author's Note
I wish to warmly acknowledge Jacob Glass for making "lots can happen" part of my everyday vernacular.

Hear Jacob on the show with me on "Freedom From Stressful Thoughts"
http://www.elesecoit.com/1/post/2009/06/jacob-glass-freedom-from-stressful-thoughts.html

Originally published as Pair #78 on 02/03/2011

To comment or read other comments online go to:
http://www.elesecoit.com/5/post/2011/02/lots-can-happen.html

The Great Unknown

Afraid to know and not know?

I read Kristine Carlson's[27] "Heart-Broken Open" and what amazes me about Kristine is her ability to remain with the unknown.

She made time to be with the heartbreak of suddenly losing her husband. She set aside space to live with it as a natural (albeit painful) part of life, to *not reject it* or force herself over the hump and eventually, in some way, to welcome it.

I find that beautiful. After all, when the unknown comes knocking we don't usually invite it in and give it a comfortable place to make camp. When life tosses us a curve ball and we wobble a bit, most often the difficult thing is that it feels like we are swinging in the dark. It is hard when we cannot see the next step. We can't see where the foot will land and how it will work out.

We've been dropped into the unknown. Usually we want out. Fast.

Of course, that's problematic. We can't get rid of things simply by ignoring or avoiding them. **So how do we live with not knowing how it will all turn out and having little power to change things sometimes?**

Often we believe we can escape by thinking our way out. We start applying lots of inner attention and we begin overthinking. We ruminate. We worry. As if we could apply enough worry to a problem to actually solve it!

This is to assume that we can find peace by intellectualizing and leaving nothing unknown, no stone unturned, no mystery unexplained.

It is as if we have lost tolerance for mystery. Even our mystery novels are tied up neatly in the end. Our scientific-driven world dislikes the unknown and the unknowable in ways that ancient civilizations did not. How will we discover something new if we can't invite the mystery of life, instead of pushing it away? When was the last time you answered a question, "I don't know?"

Personally I've really suffered from the I-should-know-by-now syndrome.

In many cases, if not all, my life would have been better served if I had let go of trying to know and found a way to allow myself to be moved and changed by what was happening. But I wanted out of the hot water as fast as I could. It's the discomfort with being uncomfortable.

So as I've fought with what life throws me, I look back and notice **I've been dragged kicking and screaming to my greatest learning experiences. All of which, I am now most grateful for.**

My question is, knowing the discomfort, how do you go at life with an open stance and open arms?

It is not easy. Kristine showed me ways I never imagined that you could grow and become more peaceful in yourself, by accepting all the feelings that arise and not trying to push them away or rationalize them.

It seems to me that the measure of peace of mind is not so much that we are in some consistent state with no moods, no ups and downs and no frenzy, but that finding peace is actually about making peace with the fact that we do have moods, we do get upset and we do get a little crazy sometimes.

That's not excuse-making, that's just being bigger than what happens to you.

Author's Note
Kris Carlson and I have a heart-to-heart talk about overcoming grief on this show
http://elesecoit.com/1/post/2011/02/grief-to-growth-with-kristine-carlson.html

And if you love living life as an experiment, listen to myself and Jen Louden[28]
http://www.elesecoit.com/1/post/2011/03/savor-and-serve-with-jen-louden.html

---

Originally published as Pair #83 on 03/08/2011

To comment or read other comments online go to:
http://www.elesecoit.com/5/post/2011/03/the-great-unknown.html

---

Please Place Your Oxygen Mask Over Your Nose and Mouth

Self Help is pretty much what it says on the tin isn't it? Helping the self.   So is that ultimate selfishness, or ultimate responsibility?

If you stop to think about it, self-help leads directly back to one's own navel pretty fast. In the midst of an "it's all about me" culture, self-help makes sense. Yet some of the most fulfilled lives have been spent considering, fighting for, writing about and trying to understand and being in service to other people.

What then, of the oxygen mask idea?   Put your own mask on so you don't snuff out before you even get the chance to assist someone else. Doesn't that suggest that selfishness is almost required before you can assist another?

About a dozen times in the last week I've also heard various people just toss out, "You must love yourself before you can love anyone else." I just wanted to stop for a moment on this one and consider if that is true.

There is certainly evidence that **helping others can be done without loving ourselves first.** Even Mother Theresa had doubts about God, her faith and her mission sometimes.

You don't need strong belief in order to help people. I've tested in my life (and asked clients to try it too) how going out and giving someone a hand when you feel a bit low can lift you. It does. So do we really need all the self-rescue before being able to lead a life that is of use to others and the world?

One of two most wonderful books ever written is by Dr. Rachel Naomi Remen[29] and called ***My Grandfather's Blessings***. Remen writes about the nature of healing, service and her work with others in counseling and treatment.

She asserts we can serve others from wherever we are: wounded, depressed and even when we ourselves are without faith or hope.

As a medical doctor with Krohn's disease she says, "I have served people impeccably with parts of myself that embarrass me, parts of which I am ashamed." (Rachel Naomi Remen, 2000, p. 198)

No self-help required, then.

Service to others does lift me, I've found. But I've also found that I can't use assisting others as my excuse to turn my attention completely away from my health, living a conscientious life, abandoning my truth or not setting boundaries.

Maybe we've just confused self-help with ridding ourselves of all defects.   And good luck with that.

Can I help others if I never any take steps to help myself?

Probably not that much.

Can I help others without being totally perfect myself?

Probably lots.

Author's Note
More on the nature of our human operating system can be heard here
http://www.elesecoit.com/1/post/2011/11/the-human-operating-system-an-upgrade.html

Originally published as Pair #34 on 05/19/2010

To comment or read other comments online go to:
http://elesecoit.com/5/post/2010/05/self-help-helps-whom1.html

Oneness and Connection

Where Is "I" and Who Cares?

Let's talk spiritual connectedness, but not as a concept. I want to talk about our very real commonality. Unfortunately, my experience is unlikely to match the directness of you seeing for yourself. Let's go there all the same.

There are many starting points to reflect on oneness and to open to seeing more deeply for oneself. Here are some that I've been offered and have found fruitful. Consider ...

- Whether human life either began with Adam and Eve or sprang from the first cell division, we would still all be, quite literally, one family all related to one another
- We were all babies once and share one experience of birth, growth and death
- We are all made up of the same matter that makes up the things that are all around us, and although the forms vary, the building blocks are the same from bricks to bones
- We are all the same because we have the same power and capacity to think
- We all share the formless energy coursing around and through us, no exceptions

You could spend time with any of these ideas and have a remarkable insight about the nature of oneness. It could change you. When I considered this more fully myself, I saw that other people don't make me feel connected; I feel connection because of what I offer to others.

I also realized that I had never met anyone in my life, I had only ever met my own thinking about a person. Look at how many people you've never met who you already love or hate — where is that happening if not within and only within you? Where is the key to connection?

Separate bodies are vulnerable, destructible, fragile and afraid of other bodies. Are we more than the sum of our body parts? And if so, how do we all partake of that? Physics is now demonstrating what spirituality has asserted for years and years: *everything is energy*.

As we question solidity itself there are fresh horizons that transcend and minimize our differences as they reveal and augment our similarities. Where would an experience of oneness arise? Our experience of the world is made in us. We make the world we see, including our sense of connection or disconnection. Considering this it occurred to me, with the thought of "I" comes with a feeling. That feeling is separateness. So if that were just a thought...?

Now I see you, now I don't

They say we never really know someone.

This weekend while I was reflecting, I realized I don't *know* anyone.

I look at others and I meet them of course. I interact with them and most of the time you'd call that getting to know them. Yet it struck me that I only know people via my thoughts about them.

I literally experience my thinking, not them. And so I create my experience of them.

But only 100% of the time.

Now if you really want to bake your noodle on this, not only do I really not know anyone but in a very strange sense, they don't even exist. Someone is standing there but my experience of them is coming from me.

Which means that **on one level, there is no "other."**

Now, I do realize that saying other people don't exist sounds a bit odd. (Just a bit.) But if it's true that we are thinking beings, thinking our way through life and that the only experience we are ever having is the experience of what is in our own mind, then it follows that we can't see anyone outside of *our thinking about them*. I mean, how could we?

So the only person I've ever met is a bunch of my own thoughts about them.

You know, isn't it true that time after time we are shocked when we find out that so-and-so had a secret lover or was embezzling or actually hates chocolate?

Have you never had the experience of talking about someone only to find out that others don't see them the way you do?

Aren't we often deeply surprised when someone very close to us reveals a secret dream or longing, or a deep desire that we had no idea about?

Don't we mainly assume people are basically like us and find it strange when they are not?

In fact we are just walking around looking at people and making them up as we go.

We are self-contained, self-referenced, meaning-makers. Except that we also assume that what we are making is *true* and real.

So, I guess there is no real like your own real.

Author's Note
Tune into Ami Chen Mills-Naim[30] and I as we discuss the principles behind life and how they play out, in particular, in our relationships

http://www.elesecoit.com/1/post/2011/05/the-three-principles-in-practice.html

Originally published as Pair #92 on 06/06/2011

To comment or read other comments online go to:
http://www.elesecoit.com/5/post/2011/06/there-is-no-one-out-there.html

It's got me all emotional. Roman Krznaric's[31] manuscript of his book: "Other People's Shoes - why empathy matters for the art of living."

It has also left me with one big question: **Have we stopped caring about caring?**

I'm not talking about how we don't act very nicely toward one another as humans inhabiting the same ground, but rather ... how is it we have come to consider it a *benefit* to be immune to the lives of others?

I'm fairly certain that we have to learn and practice how to cut ourselves off. I'm not convinced we are born this way. This process happens slowly and with method and I've even heard people justify the need for it: "You'll get hurt." "It will only cause you pain." "You'll just want to get involved." Well, yeah. Isn't that the point?

It's harder to send people to the gas chambers when you know their first names (see Schindler's List) and it's easier to be polite and leave a nice tip when you can remember waiting tables to put yourself through school.

Since when did not opening our hearts make us better human beings?

This schooling in prejudice, distance and not-my-business is one class we could really afford to skip.

As Krznaric points out, greater empathy and an openness to caring about how it feels to live the experience of another has not left us whimpering in the corner, ruined by the sheer weight of too much feeling, but in fact spearheaded the social movements that amongst other things, ended slavery.

It could be the key to why we know about the need for action on climate change but don't actually do anything about it. We won't get close enough. Remember, lack of empathy brought us the Crusades and the brutal conquest of South America.

If we are to put on new glasses today to see the world differently, why not slip on someone else's shoes too and offer ourselves the gift of deeper connection with others?

What have you got to lose except your aloneness?

Author's Note
Roman can be heard with me on the radio in the show "Empathy, the Radical Art of Living"
http://elesecoit.com/1/post/2010/04/empathy-the-radical-art-of-living.html
Roman's latest book is "The Wonderbox: Curious Histories of How to Live" (Krznaric, 2011)
and can be found here http://www.romankrznaric.com/wonderbox

Originally published as Pair #22 on 04/29/2010

To comment or read other comments online go to:
http://www.elesecoit.com/5/post/2010/04/why-do-i-care.html

How Am I?

I'm fine, You're Fine, We're All Fine

What if, for just a few minutes we actually had a conversation that was more than an exchange of "how are you" pleasantries or weather reports?

This week I thought I'd try out actually answering the questions "How are you?'" Honestly.

I don't know what will happen, really. Could be very bizarre.

I did it today, fact. I stood in line at the Post Office. It was a very long line, so you hear everyone's conversations and one of the people working today was smiling and greeting everyone with a great booming, "How Are You?"

I watched the responses. Actually, this has become so NOT a real question that some people answered, "Yeah, will this still get there by Monday morning?"

As I walked up to that particular person I checked inside. "How am I?" I wondered silently.

When it came my turn to be asked, I responded, "Actually, I'm very relaxed and quite content, thank you for asking."

It would be really nice to say that what happened next was a great moment of human connection.

Actually, he asked me if I had really been waiting my turn or cut the line. I needed to wait in line he said. Which was pretty funny, because I'd been there for 20 minutes in a very long line.

I reassured him I had waited my turn and he seemed satisfied.

Did the 20 minutes I spend checking into how I felt that make some kind of difference?

I'm thinking that maybe. It had something to do with the fact that by the time I arrived at the counter I was really, just relaxed. I was in fact, just: A woman standing in line.

What was interesting is not only that I felt good, but I also felt happy with my interaction with him. *I felt connected.* I felt connected to me and yes, to him to for a moment. Even as he questioned my personal queuing integrity.

When he said, "Have a Nice Weekend," I replied, "Well I wish that for you too."

And I meant it.

Author's Note
This radio show with Gabriela Maldonado-Montano[32] explores human conversation, interaction and what happens when our busy minds get in the way.

http://www.elesecoit.com/1/post/2011/09/meeting-of-the-minds.html

---

Originally published as Pair #13 on 04/19/2010

To comment or read other comments online go to:
http://www.elesecoit.com/5/post/2010/04/how-am-i.html

Pain

Sweet Lies, What You Get is What You See, For Those Who Have Suffered Enough

Having grown up as a Christian Scientist I have maintained a life-long interest the nature of pain and suffering. And healing.

Metaphysical and spiritual practitioners have demonstrated inexplicable healings of painful diseases. Medical science recognizes the mental component of pain. Does this mean pain is entirely mental? I don't know. I do know there is a mental element to *suffering* that is worth looking at and understanding as well as we can. For obvious reasons!

I do know I have had many experiences of my own pain being mentally caused and removed. I've also been medically and spiritually relieved of both suffering and physical pain. Also, my own clients arrive with great suffering at times and I have seen them drop their mental burdens and physical relief can follow. Yet often this can seem unsettlingly random.

Painful thinking—be it memory, passing thought, stories or beliefs—comes to life via the five senses. All human beings feel and experience whatever we think. You can't dodge that.

If you've ever seen someone worry about being sick for years and then finally end up in the hospital doesn't it make you wonder … what's worse, the operation or the years of fretting and stress that preceded it? Those worries lead to a life of suffering long before any disease arrives.

Worry is our major human disease. I believe it causes more pain than all the diseases we treat in emergency rooms and intensive care units. It is chronic, widespread and virtually untreated. In fact, it is considered an inevitable part of life as we struggle to find the true source. If you counted up the hours you have spent distressed about the state of your body, bank account or love relationships, would it not outweigh all the actual physical illness and pain you've ever seen a doctor for? Haven't you been putting up with much more mental pain than physical?

Mental suffering is so prevalent that you'd think by now we'd be seriously pursuing the root of this problem. We are not. Instead we've promulgated the myth that mental pain is caused by external factors like our jobs and the state of the economy. Viewing our mental health this way means we have little chance of predictable recovery or treatment. But you can be fine despite any external downturn if you understand the nature of suffering and the true source of your pain. If you have read this far in this book, you must already suspect where that is.

Anyone Not Suffered Enough Yet?

You want fries with that stress?

OK, it's time for a rant.

Anyone here **not** had enough of their suffering quite yet? Please stand up and go make a cup of tea.

Those still reading ... if you want to become clearer in thinking and expression (and you don't have an undiagnosed chemical imbalance) then one remedy I know is a daily dose of quietness of the mind.

You really don't even know what the roots of problems are, much less how to solve them, until you come into better control of the thought process. Now by "control" I really mean that you come to a place of ease and clarity in thinking. Not that you become the thought patrol.

Paradoxically, though, the way I had to create ease and clarity was to stop dabbling and get serious about some kind of daily reflective practice. I'm not saying you can't get a quiet mind another way. Because you can and it happens often.

But for most of us, ease can take some effort.

Sucks huh?

Look, if there is a good chance your issues are not chemical, dietary, or medical, then there is a high chance this just might work. So what it really means if you don't is simply that you really have not had enough yet.

That's harsh, isn't it?

I bet you have already been exposed to enough great methods and enough superb advice and information by now to be able to choose something that you like and that works for you as a mind-calming practice.

How about you choose the thing that helps sustains in you the greatest sense of peace, ease and focus and then commit, absolutely, to make it happen daily, no matter what. I mean that. Like, Everyday.

That's my unsolicited advice.

So how about it?

Hearing the objections in your head?

Got a really good story about why that can't happen?

Stop listening to it right now and pick up your phone.

Getting a routine going when you're not used to it can be hard for anyone, so get a daily check in buddy who you will report to. Barring that, hire a coach. Pick someone you know is going take no excuses and is going to support you lovingly and tell you the truth. I want you to pay for their great service to you.

Because if you do that, what you will be doing is telling you, finally, that you are serious.

You'll be glad you did. But maybe you won't know that for a while, so just try my advice. Feel free to curse as much as you want, but get started anyway.

Author's Note
There is nothing about a practice of any kind, be it spiritual or physical that by practice alone creates peace of mind. The source of internal peace is already within you. Dedication to recognize this and deepen this experience is not the same as becoming dependent on tools or techniques to take you there. Try what appeals to you. Be guided by your own wisdom.

Originally published as Pair #10 on 04/14/2010

To comment or read other comments online go to:
http://www.elesecoit.com/5/post/2010/04/anyone-not-suffered-enough-yet.html

---

It's not a lie, it's just not quite the truth

"Tell me lies, tell me sweet little lies"
Fleetwood Mac

Life can be painful and sometimes we are so afraid of the painful that we will do many things to avoid it.   One of the ways I noticed that I have used to avoid life's dips is lie to myself about what is going on. (If you don't' like the word "lie" substitute the words '"fool myself.")

I think we are all trying to feel better.

Even our self-fooleries are attempts to feel better.

If I know it's going to feel bad to go to the dentist, break up with someone or admit that I can't actually manage everything on my workload then I might very well tell myself that my tooth doesn't hurt that bad or that somehow things will work out.

These little trickeries don't actually work in the long run but seem as if they do in the short run. The way I can tell that I'm in the middle of a little white lie (or a big fat one) is that I actually don't feel good.

When I deal with things my life feels clear, there's nothing in the back of my head, no nagging feeling, no unexplained tiredness.

When I pluck up the guts to deal with my avoidances, my life immediately clears up and it feels like I can breathe.

If you have some little chronic pains, tiredness, lack of enthusiasm, or just a clogged up feeling inside, here are some places I look:

- Is there a conversation I'm avoiding?
- Is there an action I know I need to take that I'm not taking?

- Is there someone in my life I need to spend less time with?
- Is there a promise I made to myself I know I am not keeping?

I have found that I often don't like the answers to some of these questions.

I also notice that lying to myself and trying to pretend I don't know the answers doesn't actually work (we know the truth inside, after all).

So when we are honest with ourselves, something lines up inside that makes us feel better instantaneously.

Maybe it's our soul thanking us.

... just a thought.

Author's Note
Here's a radio show on how I learned to lessen my own suffering
http://www.elesecoit.com/1/post/2010/02/life-has-pain-and-you-dont-have-to-suffer.html

---

Originally published as Pair #28 on **05/08/2010**

To comment or read other comments online go to:
http://elesecoit.com/5/post/2010/05/lies-damn-lies-and-self-foolerie.html

---

The Film Behind The Eyes

What you see (inside) is what you get

Early in the morning I'm walking down a New York City street. I'm considering the sun and the day ahead and I'm enjoying being in a city that's strange to me. I'm having a reflective walk and a very nice experience.

Walking toward me is a woman.

We are the only two on the entire block. She looks straight ahead, she is dressed nicely, makeup on, clutching her bag across her chest.

She is walking and crying.

As we pass I can see that her eyes are very puffy and swollen and her face is wet with tears. I don't know how long she has been crying.

I immediately feel drawn to her. I remember times in my life when I have walked on the street pulling back the tears. An intense surge of compassion, love and connection fills me as we walk past each other.

As I walk on, I can still feel her. Here we are, on a NY street, no one in sight, no cars, only the morning sun on the buildings and two people walking.

What strikes me is that nothing is happening.

Nothing is happening except two people passing.

The contrast of nothing happening and this woman clearly carrying her pain tells me one thing:

She has to be playing some kind of painful thought in her mind.

There is no other possibility. All her suffering and all the tears are the response, not to the current outside environment but to her current inside one.

She is in hell right now because of the film playing behind the eyes.

How many days have we all lived in this kind of hell and our walking, crying meditation?

Author's Note
To explore more about the sources of discomfort and stress, listen to:

http://www.elesecoit.com/1/post/2011/03/the-truth-about-stress.html

http://www.elesecoit.com/1/post/2011/04/where-is-health.html

Originally published as Pair #18 on 04/25/2010

To comment or read other comments online go to:
http://www.elesecoit.com/5/post/2010/04/crying-meditation.html

Don't Jump ...

... or actually give in to the temptation to gift your children to your neighbor

... or just get in the car and drive Route 66 just to see where you end up

... or stay in bed splitting Oreos because that just sounds WAY better than a paycheck right now

curl the toes back, don't jump in the bath holding a loaded hairdryer and see if this link below won't help - it's a freebie from me - it's meant to help bring you back from the ledge

The dread truth?

It's a mess of badness out there and finally getting that new job, new partner or new President will not fix this hairball of hornets.

No matter how many times you swap out the boyfriend, lift, tuck, tan, or trim up, SOMETHING is headed your way to disturb your peace of mind.

Yet I work with people and see Mrs. "Fed Up" who can hardly stand the sight of her man and wants to tamper with his brake fluid, find peace of mind and Mr. "Rager" who's white-knuckling the steering wheel and aiming for the next brick wall, find a place in him of no-stress.

I'm supremely encouraged by this, not just because it means more people are breathing today but because it happens in the middle of life as we know it: job losses, overwork, bankruptcy, and breakdowns and it is not a gimmick.

So yes, I also have a purpose in writing this.

First, I had a crazy idea that it was possible to end people's suffering completely through some simple ideas that I teach: that you can have peace of mind and not suffer, without the world ever changing.

Please feel free to not believe me; but don't expect me to keep this to myself.

Now maybe you know someone suffering right now and you're watching and it's painful. Perhaps this audio link will help.

If you like this and it makes a difference then would you pass it on?

Someone you care about may hear something brain-crackingly important, something small and simple, but that arises from someplace inside that might fling open the exit door out of personal hell and into personal well-being.

If you really, really dig these ideas,

Spread the word.

Author's Note
The free downloadable Audio on Wellbeing - (50mins) can be found here
http://elese.audioacrobat.com/download/WellbeingInAllCircumstances_Radio2_11_11.mp3

Originally published as Pair #84 on 03/11/2011

To comment or read other comments online go to:
http://www.elesecoit.com/5/post/2011/03/before-you-rob-the-bank-marry-the-toy-boy-and-flee-to-brazil.html

---

Perfectionism and The Cult of Excellence

Hiding From Our Flaws and The Real Enemies of Brilliance

Who here does so much planning to get things just right that their writing never sees the light of day, their designs do not get crafted and their projects never get off the drawing board?

We can take the attitude toward life that it is so important to come across well, make a good impression and not blow it, that we become paralyzed. And often we don't even see this is happening. We think we are just trying to do a good job. But we are still trying to be good so mommy will love us.

The world punishes faults and foibles and people can be unkind about our mistakes, but why let that stop you? What you are trying to live up to? You fall down, people laugh, so what? You make a mistake, it gets broadcast on CNN, big deal! Unless, of course, the opinion of other people means everything to you. So far, has perfection ever guaranteed you love? If perfection is required for love then our relationships are no more than tyrannies.

Perfection is how you arrived, not what you are supposed to work hard to become. Stop looking for perfection in behaviors, performance stats and physical appearances.

Life is a dance with failure as the choreographer. We are always cracking open at the weakest point. We must stand on edge of the known and resist the urge to throw up. Self-contentment is no further than your mirror if you would ignore what you see and try to imagine who it is that is watching you look.

Humans are brilliant and silly, wonderful and scoundrels, kind and crazy – depending on what they are thinking and believing in any red-hot minute. No one has control. When was the last time you lost it? Very recently I suspect. Your secret flaws are already visible to us all and there is nowhere to hide. Yet here you are I notice, living your life regardless! No perfect human has walked the planet and never will. The paradox is, of course, that even with all our foibles and farts we are not damaged beings. Underneath our wild swings in behaviors are not differences in capacities or essence, only momentary differences in perception.

We are already perfect *with* all our imperfections. If you want to experience that, stop trying to get rid of your humanness and start trying to understand it. Suddenly you will find beauty in everyone and you will discover one day that you have dropped the need to be perfect.

Standing at the edge of the familiar ready to slay a few dragons

On the show Michael Bungay Stanier[33] I did, admittedly, go off on a wee bit of a rant.

We were chatting on the show about his book, "Do More Great Work" (Stanier, 2010). Besides the great exercises for stepping out of busy and into meaningful work, one of the things I loved about the book were the nuggets of wisdom from Michael throughout.

One that struck me in particular is that **when you are engaged in Great Work it often takes you to the edge of your known world.**

In other words you have to be courageous enough to be uncomfortable sometimes if you are going to do what really matters. It tends to stretch you beyond your competency.

Yet when we talk about "Great" or doing "Great Work" it might sound as if you are trying for some standard of excellence. Striving for a new form of perfection called Great Work. But this is not the case. You don't have to be great, or perfect, or fixed up in any way to do something meaningful.

In fact, perfectionism and what Michael termed "the Cult of Excellence" are the enemies of Great Work, precisely because **we are very unlikely to be able to both stretch into the unknown and do things perfectly at the same time.**

I love that you do not need to be a different person to make a difference.

Although, you just may need to be a fed up person who doesn't want to settle for less any longer!

Fed up just enough to keep going right to the edge of your world.

Here's one of my yellow highlights from Michael's book:

"You may have heard that when ancient mapmakers ran up to the very edge of the known world, they would write Hic Sunt Dracones, or "here there be dragons."

May we all face them more often.

Author's Note
You can hear the show with Michael Bungay Stanier here:
http://elesecoit.com/1/post/2010/05/must-you-quit-your-job-to-do-work-that-matters.html

Perfectionism is an internally generated modern plague. One of the antidotes is to learn to become more comfortable with our own humanity. Which means shaking hands much more often with the formless unknown. After all, from where else do new ideas spring?
*See also the chapter on "*Mystery, Curiosity and Wonderment.*"*

Originally published as Pair #41 on 05/28/2010

To comment or read other comments online go to:
http://www.elesecoit.com/5/post/2010/05/the-dragons-of-excellence-ate-my-shorts.html

---

Perfectly ImPerfect in Every Way

When did it get so difficult to be the learner?

It seems like never before have so many people been so uncomfortable with their own *not knowing.*

Yet when I look at my life, there isn't one single thing that I've learned that I could do perfectly the first time I tried it. None. Not:

- driving
- writing my own name
- speaking French
- walking

If you've ever said "I should have done better…" chances are you too have a little perfectionist running amok inside who thinks it's possible to get a better past through rumination and regret.

My perfectionist bully arrived when I was about 7. My first grade teacher, Mrs. Wolf had a very gnarly hand with red nails and it would swoop onto my paper as I was writing and point to the single mistake on the page. I had nightmares about her right index finger pointing the way to my certain death. I was terrorized.

I continued her practice by terrorizing myself, believing that the way to approval was through the eye of the needle of perfection.

So, are we supposed to learn by, erm, already knowing?

Just walk around to notice the number of children currently being educated in perfectionism. Why do you think so many teens commit suicide? They aren't in school to learn it seems, only to prove how much they already know. Kids do more tests, earlier, every year. Standing with your hand on the handle of the door marked Failure is terrifying and future creative lifetimes are being tossed into the waste bin right now to avoiding opening it.

What happened to when failure was considered a required class for success?

I was under the impression that mistakes are not a synonym for wasted life, but for *learning*. Someone put the wrong sign up on that door. It should say "Step through this door and experiment all ye who enter here."

Now that we are big and not terrorized by Mrs. Wolf's index finger, the Failure door shouldn't seem so scary and shameful. But it does.

Eldon Taylor[1] wrote powerfully about the "form of conditioning that can set us up for disappointment and failure ... the one that teaches us we should have an answer."

Let's take a dare together today. What if, just for today, we didn't try to be perfect?

OK, this is going to sound crazy, but you really cannot know what you don't know.

After all, what's the worse that can happen?

I can write my name, speak French, drive and walk. So worst case – you learn something.

Author's Note
You can hear Eldon Taylor on the show
 http://www.elesecoit.com/5/post/2010/04/an-open-mind-is-a-beautiful-thing.html

Hear author and comfort queen Jennifer Louden[28] (Louden, 2005) *and I talk about how to end perfectionism on this show. It's a great one!*
http://www.elesecoit.com/1/post/2010/09/ending-perfectionism-with-jen-louden.html

Originally published as Pair #5 on 04/08/2010

To comment or read other comments online go to:
http://www.elesecoit.com/5/post/2010/04/perfection-has-its-flaws.html

You Can't Hide. Period.

Nowhere to run, baby

What if you are a coach or therapist or human helper and you don't "Walk Your Talk?"

Is it bad if we can't be as good as we hope all the time? After all, we are just humans doing our best.

As I thought about this, it occurred to me that we never ask others to be perfect in order to have a conversation or to listen to us, do we?

Anyone can deeply connect with another human being and lend a listening ear. We don't say, "Well excuse me, before I talk with you I'd just like to know if you've taken care of all your own dirty laundry." On the other hand great stacks of dirty laundry eventually do begin to stink.

I bet you've encountered someone for the first time and had the experience of some sort of an odd vibe that you couldn't explain. Try as you might to connect with them, you just couldn't ... only to later discover they were promoting faithfulness but cheating on their wife or trying to get you into clean living while they hoarded old newspapers to the rafters in their own home or maybe saving animals while yelling and screaming at the neighbor's children.

I think we can sense incongruences in others. Yet how adept we are at convincing ourselves that these little things don't matter in us or that no one will know.

So do they? How do you balance your own inevitable non-perfection with your work?

For Quick Sale: One house. Glass panels throughout. Stone Garden

---

Originally published as Pair #48 on 06/09/2010

To comment or read other comments online go to:
http://www.elesecoit.com/5/post/2010/06/you-cant-hide-period.html

---

Quiet Mind and State of Mind

Making the World Flat, Brain Strain and Releasing Thoughts About Thought

Most of us intuitively know there is a link between the quality of our day and our state of mind. We know that our thinking causes stress or we wouldn't say, "That's all in your head." We now accept that the quality of our thinking has an affect on our health. Once upon a time we didn't.

At one time the mind/body connection was poo-pooed. Mindfulness centers and meditation areas in cancer hospitals would have been the stuff of science fiction. What was not medically treated was left to faith or religion with a last-ditch sigh of "We've tried everything so it can't hurt." Even today there is still a great taboo on mixing the medical and the spiritual.

As those lines blur, society now largely accepts there is a relationship between mind and experience. As a result, mind studies and disciplines have grown. Science, psychology and spirituality endeavor to describe this connection. Books abound on the nature of the mind. Some are highly technical, some wacky and some thoughtful. Yet doesn't it seem that this should be practical? We want something we can use without an expert explaining it to us.

We try to translate this into common parlance like, "It's good to relax." Which is really just common sense. (You'd be surprised, in fact to discover how much of what you can know about your own mind is simply available to you via your common sense.) We also use techniques and tools that are meant to help us settle down and take us into a quiet mind. These work. Until they don't. Ever wondered why they work some days and not all? Or for some people?

Interestingly, there is one thing that unfailingly calms the mind: Understanding.

Understanding quiets us quickly, fully and naturally. To understand how state of mind influences you is actually rather simple: start with the very fact that you are able to think. That's a power you have. Then see the nature of the thinking process, which is that you feel everything that you think. When you are feeling something, it will be completely real to you in your five senses, which is why when you dream you can sweat from fear, or if you imagine your child is in danger, your heart can pump quickly with no outside stimulus. To see this is to understand how state of mind works on you through your day and why you react as you do.

If you stick with this a bit, reflecting on the nature of mind, you also see it's possible for you to have a new thought at any time. Everyone I know who understands this begins to relax.

On Making It

Who needs rose-colored glasses?

Billy Connolly,[34] a Scottish comedian said, "there is no such thing as bad weather, only the wrong clothes."

Hm. I notice this is true. I only dislike the rain when I think it should not be raining.

And here's the interesting part ... no matter what I think about things, especially how *"I'll never make it!" or "This is it; I can't survive this"* ... I'm always making it.

Standing right where I am now, I see that I have made it through **everything** up until this moment.

You're here.

I'm here.

Nice to know.

Originally published as Pair #97 on 06/24/2011

To comment or read other comments online go to:
http://elesecoit.com/5/post/2011/06/on-making-it.html

How To Make the World Flat

You see the world however you think the world

I have some good news. Everything is in your head.

If that doesn't sound like good news, let me explain. The key to open possibility lies here.

Consider for a moment, the things around you. Whatever you look at two things happen:

1) You see it. See a lamp (ignore a wall).
2) You have a name for it.

That is another way of saying you have thoughts about it. "Lamp" may be a name we all agree on, but you still see your version. You will find a lamp pretty, ugly, misplaced or whatever.

So you actually experience the lamp (and the world) by way of your own thoughts. And thoughts show you a world of your own making. They show you the lamp "your way."

This does not mean you just imagined all the bad stuff in the world or in your life. But you do make up the filter through which you view life and that's what you might call Context. (Your pair of glasses!)

You live and move around in the context that you make. And from that context you interpret what's possible for you. See how this could be good news?

For example, in the context of "the world is flat" you would be a heck of a lot less likely to sign up for a round-the-world sailing expedition. Yet, it would be only your thoughts about a flat world that would stop you. Obviously you couldn't ever really be in a flat world just because you think that … but, isn't it fascinating you can experience a flat world as completely real all the same? We experience what we think regardless of whether it is true or not. Look how many people did!

All you have to do is think how many people ONLY ever thought of and then experienced the world as flat to see the power of thought and word to create your life. If everyone in Columbus's time came back to life right now, they'd probably try to keep you from getting on that boat.

Context tells you what's possible before you are even out the door.

And sometimes it discourages you from dangers that don't exist.

I'm in favor of relieving myself of my own and others' opinions of what's possible. Especially as I create my own context.

Creating a context by telling myself "lot's can happen," or "life is for learning" helps me have a more open-ended view of life, instead of a tapestry of limiting thoughts masquerading as truth.

Who do you need to not listen to today?

And what context would you like to create?

Author's Note
If everyone in Columbus's time suddenly came back to life, they might well try to keep you from sailing over the edge of the world, but once they knew the truth, how long would it take them to drop their old thinking? If you were going to help them, would you try to change their thinking, or would you simply show them the truth, as we know it today?

We don't really drop our thoughts; thought drops us when truth is self-evident.

Originally published as Pair #3 on 04/07/2010

To comment or read other comments online go to:
http://www.elesecoit.com/5/post/2010/04/how-to-make-the-world-flat.html

On Staying Safe (and looking under the bed)

Lions and Tigers and Bears Oh My!

I realize that our internal voice is not always very nice to us and it would seem it has some leftover primitive instincts about keeping us safe to explain why.

That doesn't mean we need to believe everything it says.

I've learned a lot recently about the brain and how it works from many of my different radio show guests, but two in particular who came to talk to me were Rick Hanson[35] and Don Goewey.[36]

Both have done separate research showing essentially that the reptilian brain, which is part of our now bigger and more complex brain, is still on the lookout for physical dangers like saber-tooth tigers and such.

One of the most fascinating by-products of this evolutionary training is that we have brains that tend to collect evidence of danger and ignore what is non-threatening.

Interesting isn't it?

I think this connects to our negative internal dialogue and becomes an integral part of the narration that goes on as we attempt to avoid danger and stay safe.

No wonder this part of our processor will tend to collect negative experiences and simply neglect to register positive ones. How many people do you know who are focused on the bad stuff?

This brain, which used to be all we had to keep us safe from all kinds of physical dangers, continues to look out for us today using its old primal impulses. That's not to say we have no way of dealing with this. There is much to know in this field.

Which reminds me, one of the ways we are often told to deal with our internal voices is to shut them up. While I've not found that I can turn off my own personal thinking at will, one tool used in visualizations is to imagine you are turning down the volume in your mind.

Now, you wouldn't want to turn down your danger voice so much that you walked right into the worst of situations. However, you really also don't need the alarm bells ringing 24/7 either.

Volume control may be an important skill when your internal dialogue is filled with negative chatter and danger warnings that lead to feelings of chronic stress. I know using this helps many.

And it also works just to simply see *there are no more saber-tooth tigers*.

Author's Note

Explore more in the radio archives as I talk to a variety of brain and mind specialists.

http://www.elesecoit.com/1/post/2010/02/why-your-brain-doesnt-cooperate-truth-about-the-mindbrain-connection.html

http://elesecoit.com/1/post/2010/03/change-your-brain-change-the-world.html

http://www.elesecoit.com/1/post/2010/02/rewire-the-brain-to-end-stress.html

Originally published as Pair #58 on 07/19/2010

To comment or read other comments online go to:
http://www.elesecoit.com/5/post/2010/07/on-staying-safe-and-looking-under-the-bed.html

This Too Shall Pass

All that effort is bad for you

Ever sat in front of your computer with a high whirring noise, hitting the keys but nothing is happening? That's what occurs when the computer is trying to process too much information all at once.

Funny to recognize those times when you are wound up in your mind in the same way.

Just like the computer that freezes up when you are most wanting to leave work or just at the end of that long project plan or term paper, the mind freezes when it is working hardest at getting an answer or making an important decision.

So then we get really wound up in our heads it all spirals downwards and gets worse.

When I work with clients on this kind of thing and they have some idea that the quality of their thinking has a role in creating the quality of their life, they see that they are freezing themselves up with the sheer numbers of thoughts going on and they often start wondering, **"How do I stop and let go of these thoughts?"**

So I just want to take a moment to realize that the instant you begin your effort to "let go" the buzz has begun ramping up again.

We all have human minds in which thoughts come and go. That's the process of thinking.

It's actually more helpful to realize that you have plenty of thoughts that you have already released and let go — today, just in the last hour. They came. They went. You hardly noticed them.

The thought that you don't want to walk the dog or feed your cat ever again might have dropped by. You just didn't feel like it. But you don't really take that seriously. You don't actually reach over to strangle the person who cuts you off in line, even if you think you want to for a split second. And then you just don't think about it anymore.

How does that happen? Did you really need to figure out how to let bad thoughts go?

You are bypassing thoughts all the time.

The nature of thought is a flow, in and out. The process itself is one that you don't have to take particularly seriously.

It's good to see that we have hundreds and thousands of thoughts in our lives (in a day!) that we have never acted on, or even come close to acting on.

That, I've found, is a really great way to not take my own thoughts so seriously.

When I worry how I will learn to let go of all my non-serving beliefs and my self-harming thoughts and I focus really, really hard trying to get rid of them it doesn't work consistently anyway.

Pick up a pen. Hold it out in front of you. Now work really hard at dropping it.

What takes effort is hanging on.

Knowing this helps.

Originally published as Pair #88 on 04/20/2011

To comment or read other comments online go to:
http://www.elesecoit.com/5/post/2011/04/this-too-shall-pass.html

---

Relationships and Intimacy

Be Nice So I Can Love You, Meeting You/Meeting Me, Princes and White Horses

Perhaps the most difficult area of for self-reflection is in relationships. We are never more challenged to look inside ourselves for an answer then when someone is standing in front of us. Especially if they are behaving badly.

The behavior of others is a primary excuse for why our own happiness is so hard to come by. Other people provide so much opportunity for blame and finger pointing that we will spend a lifetime swapping partners or jobs without ever tending to our own inner housekeeping.

The truth of relationships, no matter what others may be showing us, is that no one and no thing can get between you and you. This is sobering and liberating. It means that all relationships are completely up to one person: the person reading this.

This chapter is about seeing relationships afresh, yet firmly rooted in reality. Does that sound impossible?

Before reading on, let's pause to consider this idea of reality. What is it? If someone else inhabited your body for a day would they experience your life exactly as you do — even if they meet all the same people and do the same things you do? Or would it be different for them?

Each person sees differently, even when we look at the same things. If you share a home, a parent or work in a team and you've ever compared notes, you know two people never have the same experience of anything! Because the thoughts in each of us are totally different.

To understand that everyone literally lives in his or her own reality revolutionizes everything about relationships. Our ability to love soars as we let go of forcing people to see things our way and stand back to make room for their way. Acceptance and non-judgment is suddenly ushered in. Communication and the listening problems dissolve. And the biggest relationship killer of all, expectation, is dealt a deathblow. How can I expect anything of you? If I'm not experiencing happiness, that's me; my own thinking has to change first. It is radical to take on the part of the relationship that is your part: all of it. Because what you see is what you get.

We share a world and yet there are 6.9 billion worlds on this planet. The more I see that I inhabit my world and you inhabit yours, the more I find peace and true love with others.

How To Stay Young

Be The Fool and Live Forever

Sometimes, someone just takes the words right out of your mouth and all you can do is smile a big huge grin, bow in homage and then spread it around!

Steve Chandler[2] whom I adore, often quote and am lucky enough to know, sent a message to everyone in his Club Fearless[37] that I want to share with you below.

It fell hot on the heels of my radio show with Greg Baer[38] where we talked about how to create intimacy and in particular how much men in particular crave real intimacy.

What strikes me about the timeliness of this message is not only that I was just talking with Greg about the very same thing, but also how much intimacy and play are connected. When we are willing to be childlike and even childish, we give all those around us permission to fall down too. Our hearts melt when we see others reveal their real, quirky, kooky selves and allow us to see who they are. It is the only way to create the distinct possibility of being accepted — silliness and all.

And it could be pretty fun too.

Here's to your wonderful, playful, grass-stained-knees weekend!

From the desk of Steve Chandler:

"'To keep your marriage brimming,
With love in the loving cup,
Whenever you're wrong, admit it;
Whenever you're right, shut up.'

-Ogden Nash, author (1902-1971)[39]

This applies to all relationships. Relationships are split apart by our ego's love of 'winning' and 'being RIGHT!'

Look for a chance to make a fool of yourself. Be wrong. Don't be afraid to lose face and fail. Don't reject the idea of coming across as a human being. Jump in. Play. Fall down. Get up. Play harder. Come home with a dirty face and sweat on your neck. Take a bath. And sleep. You lived life that way when you were young.

Forever young,

Steve"

Author's Note
I talk with Steve Chandler about how to live a fearless life:
http://www.elesecoit.com/1/post/2009/08/how-to-live-the-fearless-life-with-master-coach-steve-chandler.html

The show with Greg Baer, on What Men Really Want can be heard here:
http://elesecoit.com/1/post/2010/06/what-men-really-want.html

Greg and I also explore Radical Honesty and Real Love in this radio show:
http://elesecoit.com/1/post/2010/03/radical-relationship-healer-truth-telling.html

---

Originally published as Pair #46 on 06/05/2010

To comment or read other comments online go to:
http://www.elesecoit.com/5/post/2010/06/how-to-stay-young.html

---

Imaginary Relationships

He's Just Not That Into You

One of the things that has most brought me crashing to the floor in my romantic relationships is that I tended to see what I want for me about people, rather than actually letting them show me who they are.

The very best way to fool oneself is to focus on the things about the other person that most meet our own needs rather than taking in the whole person in front of us.

If you've ever found yourself married to say, an obsessive compulsive, chances are that the signs were there in week #1, if not on the first date.

An open attitude of discovering another requires withdrawing the agenda a bit and taking more notice of what's right in front of us. I suspect it's also greatly helped by being open in yourself, being open to them and then not taking the whole thing so damn personally.

In dating, think simple and obvious: if someone is saying that they are interested in seeing you, what usually happens is they make time to see you.

How many girlfriend conversations do we need to figure that out? All you have to do is notice. And carry on living your wonderful life.

Speaking as a woman, I think we girls will be much happier if we take notice of what's there and don't take things so personally. Don't make excuses for why he's not showing up and why he's not calling. That's just what *you* want to happen. Wanting things to be different when they are not is a recipe for suffering.

Give that up in favor of noticing that what is actually going on.

It's so much kinder on you.

As Byron Katie says, *"Reality is what it is. How do I know I want to stand up? I'm standing."*

The way I know someone wants to talk to me is they get in touch.

The way I know that someone wants to see me is they are here.

In the end, if you let reality show you the way, it's not nearly as complicated as what we tell ourselves. There is very little to figure out.

Just a process of seeing.

And then you can use the energy you saved for something else.

Author's Note
For a collection of radio shows on the topic related to Love and Relationships visit my Radio Page
http://elesecoit.com/past-shows.html

Or see a list here:
http://elesecoit.com/1/category/love%20relationshipsa22e2c5ac4/1.html

Originally published as Pair #23 on 05/01/2010

To comment or read other comments online go to:
http://www.elesecoit.com/5/post/2010/05/imaginary-relationships.html

Everybody Wants to Rule The World

Standing outside and looking in on the lives of our friends and family makes it so very easy to see what is wrong with them! We can see exactly where they are messing up, we can see what they need to fix and we have the answers for what they should do next ...

... or do we?

Recently I got very convinced I had someone else's answers. It was a sobering moment.

I had to ask myself, how could I know for certain this person should exercise, lose weight, rest, relax, meditate, read or do anything else? How can I possibly know that?

It all seemed so reasonable. I was convinced I was right. Dare I say, righteously so.

Then I stepped back to realize that my good advice has no basis whatsoever, no matter how sensible it sounds.

I had to admit that **what I was really saying was "I know better than you. You should relinquish your free will and use mine."** That's ludicrous. No, it's more than that, it's actually damaging to the other person.

Even if someone manages to diet, relax, and lose weight or whatever — what have I actually taught them? I've only demonstrated that they can't trust their own good sense and that their own opinion doesn't count for much. Not to mention me revealing my low opinion of them. So low in fact that, I don't consider them capable of making their own decision but rather only capable of following mine! That's quite insulting. I would hate to be in such relationship with my coach, friend or parent.

Let's be clear. I have also encouraged them to relinquish the one thing worth having: their own wisdom. And with it went their power of choice and the ability to experience the consequences of their own actions.

Without that, how can you know you are the actually the only one responsible for how your life turns out?

After all, this is where the good news begins.

How can I ever know enough about your life to have a sound basis for advice?

How do I know that your imminent heart attack won't be the final straw that reunites you with your estranged children?

How can I predict what will finally help you draw the line in the sand under a life of substance abuse?

How do I know what is best for you **ever**?

I simply can't know. That is the plain, ego-deflating truth.

And so my so-called good advice may well be something you can do without.

Originally published as Pair #64 on 08/02/2010

To comment or read other comments online go to:
http://www.elesecoit.com/5/post/2010/08/my-plan-for-everyone.html

---

Peek-a-boo, I don't see you

Everyday I meet people who I've never seen and don't know. Everyday I also see people who I have met and also don't know – but I think that I do.

Have you ever noticed that there seems to be a point we decide that we know someone well enough to stop taking in new information about them? On what do we base this? Does it relate to how many times we've seen them? Is it based on the number of heart-to-heart talks we have had?

This point seems to arrive for all relationships including our most intimate ones, family members and friends.

It's almost as if the longer they stand in front of us the less we see them.

I think it does take a certain conscious effort to come to know someone. When I give someone my attention, listen and spend time with them – that is all time spent in an exchange between two people. **More often than not that exchange is less for the purpose of coming to discover someone and more for the purpose of trying to figure the other person out.**

I'm wondering about this.

For example, after all these years, do I really listen to who my mother is today or do I still listen to her as if she were the same person I "knew" growing up?

Am I open to discovering her? Or am I more interested in feeling that I have her figured out?

If I make a conscious effort at anything, surely it should be to drop my ideas about someone, to open my mind so that I can take in new information about them.

So I can see them.

If I am not willing to rediscover people on a daily basis, that means is the more I know someone the less likely I am to actually see them.

The ironic thing about all of this, of course, is that I myself (and each of us, I think without exception) want to be seen. We all want to be truly seen and heard.

That's impossible if our daily interactions are about deductions rather than discoveries.

What might we discover about someone we love if we just allowed ourselves to wake up one morning and pretend we don't really know them at all – and just let them show us who they are?

Author's Note
What would it take to drop our notions and concepts about all people, and come fresh to the world?

Originally published as Pair #15 on 04/21/2010
To comment or read other comments online go to:

http://elesecoit.com/5/post/2010/04/not-seeing-the-person-in-front-of-you.html

Someday My Prince Will Come. Not.

Being Cinderella blows

A message to those waiting for prince charming...

Give it up.

Not that there isn't someone out there for you. Not that you don't have a soul mate. Not that you will always be single because you live in a town with more penguins than eligible men, or you are too old, too fat or anything else.

The terrible truth is that the person that will save you is not coming because no one in the whole wide world can intervene between you and yourself.

Are you talking yourself down in the mirror every day, but then expecting someone to come and find you gorgeous? Are you repeating to yourself how unhappy you feel about your life or your singledom and then expecting someone to come and zap you into happy town?

The person that will fix the unhappiness, the person that will make you feel loved when you are mean as hell to yourself, the person that will make everything alright — THAT person is not coming. He or she is not looking for you right now. They are not just a vibration away. They are not coming.

And thank goodness for that. Because life starts when we give up the desire to be rescued.

Originally published as Pair #20 on 04/27/2010

To comment or read other comments online go to:
http://www.elesecoit.com/5/post/2010/04/someday-my-prince-will-come-not.html

Self Love and Self Care

Recipe For Self Care, You Are The Gift and Self-Help Helps Whom?

I have many wonderful clients and I'm sure you know many tremendous people, who have made choices that are not in their best interests. Many times clients tell me that the way out of such poor decision-making is to learn to love themselves more. Now, at first this made sense to me, as you'll see in these articles. Today, I'm not so sure.

"Love yourself" is a self-help assignment meant to undo all the ways we have practiced bashing and berating ourselves. Now, in contrast to being self-punishing, being self-loving is a big improvement. After all, it feels rather good when you stop punching yourself in the face.

At the same time, as far as lasting effects go, I see many people doing self-supporting things and still not feeling more accepted, loved, loving or lovable. That included me. So the more I looked at this learned self-love, the less sense it made to me. Here's why ...

You would never have to tell a child to learn to love him or her self. That's simply ridiculous. Children are beings of pure love. They love life. They love play. They love others. They dig themselves already. We all arrive on this planet as little love bursts set up to explode naturally into full individuals with no help from anyone. We are born whole and wholly loving. We get on with it. We don't begin life on earth by needing an appointment with the therapist.

Many of my own self-care practices, while intended to give me greater grounding, revolved around me trying to love and approve of my persona. Personas are things we make up as we go along in life and we have a lot invested in them. We identify with them. So much so we almost forget we've done it. We get amnesia about the fact that they are constructs. Learning to love a personality you've built in order to interface with the world is a waste of your time. Personalities aren't that lovable. But what's underneath is: It's you. Not you the personality, but you as you arrived here — childish glee and glowing lovability intact.

We can never "get" love because love is what we are. It is what I am. It is the undamaged and unblemished core of each of us. It is our base metal. You can't change that and you cannot "become" that. You already ARE that. A brick doesn't learn to be a brick.

Today my most self-loving practice and the best form of self-care I know, if you want to call it that, is reflection. It's seeing what is behind things and letting them reveal themselves. In deeper reflection I realized that Love doesn't have to learn to love itself.

Different inside and out?

Reading Ali Campbell's[40] book *"Just Get On With It!"* reminded me how important it is to take a moment to become aware of the way our minds can work to sometimes sabotage our best laid plans (and lives!) and just how much we can actually do about it.

Ali has a great exercise where he suggests the following:

"I want you to imagine that everyone around you can hear your thinking. Imagine that everyone can hear your every thought ... How different would you be?"

How horrified we'd be if others could hear us and how different we are on the inside compared to what we try to portray on the outside.

Ali is pointing out the conflict we create inside ourselves and goes on to explain how to find your way through a conflicted, overthinking mind.

The reason I like this, and his book, is because when you actually picture and hear the kinds of things that you say to yourself on a regular basis something else happens too ...

You realize how mean you are to yourself.

Most of us tolerate saying things to ourselves that we would never, ever tell a small child: how stupid we are, how useless we are, how pointless things are.

If our constant internal diarrhea would be embarrassing or unpleasant to speak out loud, just imagine the damage it's doing! And of course, it's not "it" doing this. It's actually us.

If you can't speak your inner dialogue aloud, why are you saying it at all?

I want to hear a really good reason.

Author's Note
My show with Ali Campbell can be found here
http://elesecoit.com/1/post/2010/6/-more-of-what-you-want-fast-and-less-of-what-you-dont.html

---

Originally published as Pair #54 on 06/28/2010

To comment or read other comments online go to:
http://www.elesecoit.com/5/post/2010/06/innies-and-outies.html

---

Renew Your Subscription To Yourself

Today is just a quick reminder to check in on self-care.

For me, that is!

Self Care is a practice I have come to take seriously for one reason: Whenever something in my life is going wrong, I'm not handling something well or things just appear to be going generally nutso, my self care has almost always slipped.

In my case it will be either that I'm not doing what I know nourishes me or, I'm doing it, but only half-heartedly.

When I say "self care" I mean more than physical exercise. I mean my own daily commitment to sit quietly, to read, to get in touch with what I'm grateful for and at the moment, to also do one of the daily lessons from A Course in Miracles.[41]

I do physical exercise too, and yes, if that slips my mind gets a bit duller and I feel tired and lackluster. Exercise is great, all forms, strenuous and gentle. I've come to appreciate the need for excellent care and feeding of the body!

At the same time, if physical exercise is my only form of self-care, I find it's not enough. I need spiritual nourishment and a mental resting place each day.

What do you need/enjoy/appreciate/thrive with?

More importantly, how will you know and where will you look to find out?

How will you recognize the right answer for you?

So as James Taylor sings:

"If you're down
and troubled
and you need some love and care
and nothing,
nothing is going right
close your eyes..."

... and think of your self care.

Author's Note
It was thoughtful intention around my own self-care that helped me to see more deeply about the nature of self-care – not only as practices but as reflection and introspection.

Originally published as Pair #27 on 05/07/2010

To comment or read other comments online go to:
http://www.elesecoit.com/5/post/2010/05/caring-for-the-self.html

Should-ing all over yourself

Self Care? Oh, I highly recommend it.

For me.

However, for about 20 years I tried (um, read "failed") to establish a regular routine of either yoga or meditation or both. I had heard about and believed in both as good things I could do for myself. My very earnest attempts at this however, are best summed up **not** under the heading The Art and Science of Self Care but rather as Elese's Awesome Intentions and Marvelous Wishful Thinking.

My self-care rallying cry was, "I really should do this."

I hear this a lot from clients who come for coaching. We will delve into an area of their life that isn't working and it will become clear that the reason they are feeling increased stress or are suddenly less able to maintain their cool with the kids, is because they are already on empty and not taking good care of themselves. When they realize they've not been going for walks, not reading, not singing or whatever it is that nourishes them, usually the first thing out of their mouths is, " *Yeah, I know, I really should do this.*"

Now, that may be perfectly true. Maybe they should. Whatever that means. I thought I *should* meditate but that never helped me to actually create a regular practice. Here's the skinny as far as I'm concerned:

- Everyone who has a gym membership and doesn't go, tells themselves they should
- Everyone who wants to take vacation and doesn't, tells themselves they should
- Everyone who has an addiction at some point, tells themselves they shouldn't

"Should" and "shouldn't" may sound accurate or appropriate (especially when it comes to over-eating and exercise) but **they just don't work** to make us do anything. They do work really well to make us feel bad though! And from what I see, I can never feel bad enough about something to make myself do it.

Fast forward to today.

For the past many years I've had a daily meditation practice of 20 minutes, sometimes 40, 10 or 5 minutes, but I rarely miss a day. How did I do that? I suppose I started taking notice of what my life was like when I did it, and what it was like when I didn't. No big deal really.

I noticed how much easier my day was when I did meditate. I tuned into that without really trying to make myself do it and then apparently I just continued. I continue to continue, I've noticed.

My recipe for doing something you are avoiding but that you think will nourish you, support you and make your life easier? Observe.

Notice your life with it. Notice your life without it.

Think of it as a Science Experiment.

You'll find your answer. It will be the perfect one for you.

Author's Note
If you'd like to try something different, listen to my show with Genpo Roshi[42] as he walks me through the "Big Mind" process, which he has further developed since the book "Big Mind, Big Heart." (Roshi, 2007)
http://www.elesecoit.com/1/post/2010/02/zen-meditation-on-speed-dial.html

---

Originally published as Pair #40 on 05/27/2010

To comment or read other comments online go to:
http://www.elesecoit.com/5/post/2010/05/self-care-recipe-remove-should-and-stir.html

---

You are the gift

My gift to you

The best gift you can give others is to have your own life work.

The best gift you can give to others is to realize they are not you.

The best gift you can give to others is to keep your advice to yourself.

The best gift you can give to others is all of yourself.

The best gift you can give to others is ...

... What do you think?

Originally published as Pair #80 on 02/16/2011

To comment or read other comments online go to:
http://www.elesecoit.com/5/post/2011/02/you-are-the-gift.html

Stress and Worry

I've Got Weather, Our Kids Are Not Alright, Recipes for Disaster, Money Woes

If we are going to resolve stress, we'd better be clear about where it comes from. According to literature, there are as many causes of stress as there are human situations: the workplace, your last paycheck, your test results, your genetic type, death in the family … anything.

Yet despite the apparent infinite number of stressors, there is a curious truth: the same situation will not necessarily cause stress in every person. In fact, exactly the same thing will not always cause the same response in the same person. What "stresses you" today may not tomorrow or may get worse. We know one thing only: there is no predicting what kinds of things will cause what in anyone. Period. Why? Because things don't cause stress at all.

The truth is that human stress is not created by any person, place or thing but by our own individual thoughts about these things. This does not mean your mind is sick. All it means is that if you really want rid of stress you must understand where it lives or your solutions will fail. And they have, haven't they? To crack this nut, we must look at human inner mechanics.

The source of stress, worry or any other negative (or positive) emotion is always the same: inside not outside. Feeling is subject to human engineering law: we feel whatever we think.

Another way to say this is thinking comes alive in us through our five senses. So much so, that we do not need to be in the jaws of danger in order to be afraid, nor do we need to be looking disaster in the face to feel dread or sadness. We can and do conjure the full spectrum of human feeling both with and without immediate physical or visual queues or sources of any kind.

Thinking flows fast through the human receptor and is picked up by our awareness, activating the ability for thinking to come alive within us. To visualize this, pretend you are a movie projector. If the scary film is on and the projector plugged in, what is the film we see? A scary one. Obviously! Will we be scared watching it? Probably, yes, but only while that scene is showing. In a film, we expect that. When it comes to mind-films, however, we forget. We forget precisely because of the law working within us that allows them to come to vivid life.

Each human being inhabits their own feeling world that is utterly indivisible from the thoughts behind it. Like the projector illuminating a film. Thoughts come to life within us, whatever they are. What makes the biggest difference with stress or any negative feeling then, is not so much to get busy changing our film, but to understand that we are the projector.

I've got weather

Is the internal forecast mostly cloudy?

Before I got out of bed this morning I could hear the wind and rain. As I sat with my tea, with the rain blowing sideways and the sky looking distinctly unfriendly, I realized with curiosity ...

... it hadn't occurred to me to be upset.

In that moment I saw that I was perfectly content and I had no concern whatsoever that this storm would never finish or that the sun will never come out again.

It just didn't cross my mind. Or if it had, I had missed it.

When I talk about the nature of our internal weather, our emotions and our thinking, people often tell me we have habitual thoughts that hold us back and that it is hard to change.

My answer is well, the last time you thought about killing someone, did you actually do it?

The fact is, we think. We are thinking our way through life. And the fact is we are also ignoring some of our thinking all the time.

We are living in an internal weather system of thought.

Isn't it interesting that we worry that thought storms will never pass?

Originally published as Pair #81 on 02/23/2011

To comment or read other comments online go to:
http://www.elesecoit.com/5/post/2011/02/ive-got-weather.html

The Kids Are Not Alright

There's no harm like self-harm

I am not sure it will shock any of you to know that we are raising a new generation of stressed-out kids.

What I didn't know was the depth of where they go to release that stress. I think I imagined the reasons why a child might reach for pills and alcohol. What I did not imagine was stressed out kids *who think that a viable option for dealing with stress is through harming themselves.*

They call this de-stress practice: "cutting."

As I researched the topic for the show on The Truth About Stress, I discovered a dark fact on the forums and boards on the Internet. There are children of 12, 13, 15, screaming for help to find a way out of their stress, writing:

"I'm stressed OUT and I don't know what to do! I've tried everything - I've been cutting myself to relieve the stress."

Cutting themselves? To relieve stress? At 12 years old?

My heart beat in my throat as I read those almost exact words many times over.

And here is the worst part. Knowing what we know about how stress is created and how it does not come from something outsides ourselves, just **imagine** cutting yourself to relieve the pain of your own thoughts! It's like thinking you need to shoot yourself with one hand so you'll stop hitting yourself with the other.

Cutting, drinking, and drugs — all the myriad of "solutions" being applied to the everyday problem of hugely over-wrought thinking.

Let's understand the nature of our own minds so we stop using them against ourselves.

I'm not suggesting that any of us are harming ourselves because we are somehow wrong or stupid. Each of us who are older realize we too, had our journey to come to understand the nature of life, to take distance from our problems, to look at things from that shade outside of ourselves before we could see anything differently. Now we have our own children. Look what we are passing on to them.

Some of these children will never get perspective on their problems over the natural course of a life because they will give up hope long before then and give up on life.

Is it hard to remember the days when GPA was EVERYTHING, when getting into the University of your choice felt like a matter of LIFE AND DEATH, and if you broke up YOU WOULD NEVER LOVE AGAIN? These dramatic, all-or-nothing beliefs were part of our thinking too at one time. Now we know better. Or do we?

As I shared my love, care, my experience and my perhaps more philosophical point of view with some of these young people I wondered, how many of us have mastered our own understanding enough to really teach the children?

By the responses, I'd say we are failing to. And what will happen if we don't? I shudder.

Then I remember why I do what I do.

Author's Note
More on the topic of stress in the radio archives
http://www.elesecoit.com/1/post/2011/03/the-truth-about-stress.html

And ... my show on "Spiritual Parenting" with Ami Chen Mills-Naim[30]
http://elesecoit.com/1/post/2009/08/3-principles-for-spiritual-parenting.html

Originally published as Pair #87 on 04/12/2011

To comment or read other comments online go to:
http://www.elesecoit.com/5/post/2011/04/the-kids-are-not-alright.html

I'm not digging the stress, man...

What is your preferred stress relief: alcohol? Medication? Exercise? Therapy? Or, all of the above? I bet we have all pretty much tried them all, maybe not simultaneously — or at least not as far as I remember.

Ultimately we do them all, alone or in combination, but interestingly they don't actually work. I'm coming to believe that is because stress doesn't actually exist. It's not a thing. Stress can't be thrust upon you and no one can give it to you. Even what other people do can't make you stressed.

That is not to say that if you take a drug meant to reduce anxiety, it doesn't work. It does. I've seen it. Drugs that remove anxiety work well and help you feel like everything is fine. That doesn't make everything fine. It just makes you less aware. That could be good. And that might not be so good in some cases.

To feel stress or anxiety, you need to be narrating the events you are seeing (feel free to test this out and see if it's true). You have to be telling yourself *something*. And generally it sounds like this:

This should not be happening to me. (But it is)
They need to stop this right now. (But they don't)
I used to be able to do these things. (But right now I can't)
I should definitely have this handled by now. (Why don't I?)

One example of this is someone said to me the other day "I can't stand this anymore." But the reality was that in fact, there they were, standing in front of me "standing it." They weren't happy about it and it wasn't fun. There was a lot of physical discomfort but in reality, they were standing it perfectly.

I am not saying pain doesn't exist. It does. I'm just saying we have trained ourselves to narrate our own lives and maybe we'll never stop, but we can stop ignoring the fact we are doing it.

Now, I just want to confess, if I'm in terrible pain, I might very well take a pill. I might need enough relief to think more clearly. I do what I can do and I'm not a doctor, healer, or a spiritual practitioner who does prayer treatments.

It's just very nice to know that whatever happens, it's possible to manage my own stressful thinking without a cocktail.

If I so chose.

Originally published as Pair #65 on 08/05/2010

To comment or read other comments online go to:
http://www.elesecoit.com/5/post/2010/08/whose-recipe-for-disaster-is-this.html

Easy Money

What's in Your Wallet?

With Michael Neill[8] joining me on the show and Money as our topic, I've been thinking ...

how's my relationship with money these days?

Many of us have a bi-polar relationship with money. When we have it we worry we will lose it. When we don't have it, we worry we never will. And somehow no matter how much we have, it never seems to be enough.

Quickly take your money temperature:

- How much of your time is spent thinking about money?
- How much of your energy will be spent today worrying about money?
- How many days or months has that been the case?

A few years ago I'd have run a high fever on those questions.

I tortured myself with money worries and then (and with some good help from Michael actually) I got better at seeing the difference between my situation and my thoughts about it. I saw that my mind was tied up in worry and I was living in a disaster film of my own creation.

Once I stopped doing that, I freed up my creative mind.

I can't tell you how to become a millionaire, but I can tell you this: I never solved any problem by applying worry to it.

I solve problems by "relaxing my attention off the problem" and not taking my own thinking so seriously and then acting on good ideas when they arrive.

It is possible to use your vivid imagination to formulate your next step rather than just allowing it to create disaster scenarios in a daily loop. This took me a bit of practice to do at first, but you'll get the hang of it.

It means you can have an easy relationship with money.

And everything else.

Author's Note
The show with Michael Neill can be heard here:
http://elesecoit.com/1/post/2010/05/wave-goodbye-to-money-fear.html

Originally published as Pair #26 on 05/05/2010
To comment or read other comments online go to:

http://elesecoit.com/5/post/2010/05/easy-money.html

Wants, Desires and Addiction

Permission To Want, Shop Till You Pop, Stuff and More Stuff, Wanting v Desire

Have you ever come across something in your home you'd purchased but actually forgotten to unwrap? Ever given away brand new, never-used items to charity that you paid good money for? Ever REALLY wanted something badly, got it and then moved straight to the next thing?

Everyone has done this in some form and that's no big deal, but for me it was an everyday thing. I had a shopping addiction. It cost me a lot of money. It also taught me a great deal.

I cannot speak for all addictions but although I indulged mine often, satisfaction eluded me. The compulsion was ever-present, voracious and always on the hunt. Yet I would have said I was a normal, fairly happy person with a job. I did not consider myself crazy or addicted.

This had led me to explore an interesting distinction between wanting things versus being a human being with desires. It is not always so clear when healthy desire has been supplanted by craving. So much of our wanting is fused with our self-esteem and personal identities.

I wanted to understand the difference between wanting and desire in my bones and be forever free of addiction – and to be free of chastising, controlling or being chained to abstinence.

When one explores the true nature of desire, it's interesting that you will find no craving in it. The upwelling of desire is brimming with joy and happy to be here – whether fulfilled or unfulfilled. It loves to be and it is curious about what's possible. It gives directions but is elastic. Impossible, strange, ridiculous and slightly loopy are perfectly acceptable, simply because desire is the path by which your own uniqueness explores itself. Desire does not consider itself the destination. Desire does not "need." Desire does not cling, possess or hoard. If it has any compulsion at all, it would be to come alive.

Perhaps you inexplicably adore pandas and sailing and oysters. Someone else loves learning Chinese, donut-making and Scrabble. Our human mosaic of desires is infinitely variable and it is gorgeous. It has created our greatest inventions and is measured by our what-the-heck-ness.

If you had no desire you would not be you. Perhaps you would not even be.

To learn the difference between craving and true desire is to never again confuse insatiable appetite with self-expression. It is our constant lesson in pure happiness.

Dying To Shop

Being in NY for Supercoach Academy[3] every month gives me lots of opportunities to eat out, walk, people watch and shop.

And shop.

Shopping is an old pastime of mine.

No, let's be completely honest — shopping was a big addiction and a large part of my life.

Just like anything of this nature, alcohol, sex or any other pastime that hangs around, it's all about looking for things to feel better. We think the things create the good feelings so it's natural to go seeking stuff that "makes us feel good."

But no matter what the compulsion, many of us have started to notice that it doesn't actually work for the purpose intended. At least not in the long term. It just moves the pain around for a while.

If you consider the way we learn to think about the world: that pleasure comes from having and getting things, safety comes from protecting ourselves against horrible things, this is all very understandable. And frankly, for some of us, it will take reaching the very end of the rope of endless seeking before we even start to consider that viable alternatives might exist.

I do think we have a longing for something in life.

I don't think that is the same thing as nagging insatiable desire.

It is a tragedy to confuse the two.

Once you come to believe that happiness can only lie in satisficing desires, you are doomed to a life that is driven by acquiring and then the real tragedy emerges: **it is not so much that we can't ultimately get what we seek, but the looking back on life and realizing you've wasted it**

seeking something you didn't need.

I don't think a closet full of clothes would make up for that.
Somehow.

Author's Note
The idea of Getting and Protecting Behaviors was shared with me by author and teacher Greg Baer. (Baer, 2003)

You can hear us talk about Relationships and Truth Telling on this show:
http://www.elesecoit.com/1/post/2010/03/radical-relationship-healer-truth-telling.html

Originally published as Pair #17 on 04/23/2010

To comment or read other comments online go to:
http://www.elesecoit.com/5/post/2010/04/shop-till-you-drop.html

All is Never Enough

I can understand that we want stuff. I want stuff.

I want to have things, I want to feel things, and I want experiences as well as stuff.

Stuff is great and it's fun.

You can eat it, play with it, climb it, build with it and take it for a drive. It's just a really crap way to find happiness when we feel empty.

Our human paradox or curse or whatever you want to call it is that, having no experience of a sense of happiness arising from the inside, we look outside to find it. Unfortunately "finding" happiness outside of ourselves isn't possible.

That's just a fact. It's simply impossible.

I don't know about you, but I have looked!

Most of us will look outside, sometimes for a long time, before we become ready to turn inward. Just the fact we are looking shows we know nothing about it. Sometimes it is only the disappointment that arises out of great avarice or great loss that may finally teach someone that no amount of things (money, love, sex or Anything) will ever be the true key to happiness.

In that sense greed may be a bizarrely good thing that accelerate a normally slow process of discovering the emptiness of things.

When we don't understand that happiness already lies within us, this is just what we tend to do. It's also what we've been taught by everyone around us to do.

Excess is also a good teacher.

Some of us need to go to excess in something, or many things, in order to find the boundaries of it for ourselves. When we go to excess in the acquisition of things it simply has the same ending point: to teach us there is no satisfaction here.

We all learn that lesson in our own ways. Who can say who has the best way?

But you don't win the game if you are the one with the most toys when you die.

Author's Note
There is no key to happiness. Because there is no "TO happiness."

Originally published as Pair #51 on 06/14/2010

To comment or read other comments online go to:
http://elesecoit.com/5/post/2010/06/wanting-stuff.html

Wanting vs Desire

Wanting says it all

Our *wanting* is a huge black hole of never-enoughness but *desire* is the sign of a healthy human.

Wanting is excessive by nature. It is never is filled up and it always wants, by definition, more. It underpins our constant state of unhappiness, all our striving, our personal masks and our poor choices. It can be personal hell on earth.

Yet in principle, there is nothing wrong with wanting. So why the hub-bub?

I think as we see so much of our wanting leading to greater unhappiness we've drawn the bizarre conclusion that wanting is bad. It's not. We all have permission to have what we want and to have it. As I thought about this more, I found myself exploring the differences between wanting and desire.

When I say desire, I am not talking about desire as in our sexual appetite, but rather that personal heart-GPS device, an internal compass, an inkling, an inner urging of "let's go over there."

Desire is the walking across the street to smell a flower.

It's the signing up for a children's literature writing class when you don't know why.

It's knowing what you want for lunch.

What I notice is that desire takes me to places where I am often free of wanting anything.

Desire doesn't make me feel better. It just simply feels good. If I don't get it, I'm not hurt, disappointed or miserable.

Is this distinction making sense?

Here is another thing: I do not have to deserve anything when it comes to desire. I just follow it or I don't.

Wanting is the path of those who believe in worthiness.

My wish for all humanity is that everyone get far, far, far, more than they "deserve." We don't deserve, but we do express.

Desire gives expression a destination.

Originally published as Pair #49 on 06/10/2010

To comment or read other comments online go to:
http://www.elesecoit.com/5/post/2010/06/wanting-vs-desire.html

---

Well-being, Health, and Identity

Peace Includes Not-Peace, Recipe for Better Everything, and No Self-Improvement

Human beings have bodies and minds and live in a wide variety of fluctuating emotional, mental and physical states. It is helpful to understand how these states come about so that we can locate the unproductive ways we try to manipulate and manage our lives. But of course, what people ultimately want is to feel happy, feel well and thrive. It's what people hire me for.

People who get coaching often expect strategies, advice, tips, tools and techniques that will take them to these desirable states. When I began my search I also wanted these things and as I went along I measured my development against my ideal — who I would be when I was ALL better. When I "got there." That is, the place I'd be after so much fixing that no more fixing would be required ever again. I thought I would arrive at my well-being by working at it.

But I missed the beginning of the story: arrival day one, gate one, July 27, when I emerged perfectly ready and perfectly equipped for my life, well-being intact. I came preloaded knowing how to love, learn and heal. Nothing missing. I am using those capacities now to write these words. These arrived with me the day I was born. Where I needed to look was back at the start.

As I went along in life I also forgot I do not live in a void. I am connected to a living system. This is true not just on a biological level and on the quantum physics level of super-string, but on a very personal level. I am in aliveness and when I am not trying to improve on that I have great feeling of happiness, clarity and peace and a keen intuitive sense of what is right for me.

We are part of a living grid and as we breathe, move, think, feel and look around, Life cannot be fully seen. We see the forms life takes but Life itself is beyond and before those shapes. Life's energy is moving through, invisibly animating everything. Including you and me. You know this if you have ever had a change of heart or a new idea "out of the blue." An idea takes shape.

We are blind to this source of ourselves, the part that is not visible, untouchable, unbreakable, whole and complete. We already are ultimate well-being. You can experience all sorts of thoughts about not being enough but when those pass and you are fine again, you see you cannot misplace what you are. The gift of being you is yours to keep whether you see it or not.

You could call it your natural Self, your innate self, your authentic self or whatever you like but there's one thing: it certainly doesn't need to go out and get well-being, wellness or health. It already has them. And more.

You are the one you've been looking for

What can other teachers do?

If they don't know for themselves, they are just swallowing other people's saliva.

- Yun-Men

Enlightenment. Sometimes I think the word should come with instructions and a Surgeon General's label. *"Warning. May cause extreme bloating of ego."* Or, *"Warning, May cause sanity defects."*

The reason I think striving for something called enlightenment is so damaging to one's health is that it sends us into paralysis. It is the disease of the seeker, who must by necessity seek. Maybe we'll wave a quick hello to acceptance, rest and peace as we dash down the road toward the destination called Somewhere Better.

There is no need to put off anything until such a time as we become a better person, a holier person, or a more enlightened person.

I realized that I will not find love, be able to help people more, make more money, or change the world when I am all fixed up. Being fixed up isn't required. In fact, the last person I want to come and help me, frankly, is that perfect person (you know the one!).

Only an ego puffed on self-importance could ever think up the idea that you must be in a high place before you can engage fully and be of assistance to others. What better mechanism to keep a narcissistic, self-absorbed, know-it-all ego firmly in place than the concept of an enlightened state, which will be reached someday in the future.

What will we do with our "higher state" after all? Help people? Oh my goodness. People should run from us as quickly as they can screaming, "Run, here comes someone with The Truth!"

Now I do think it is worth looking for and finding your truth. I have found it is also valuable to cultivate self-awareness. (I had to learn that was not the same thing as self-perfection, but that's another story).

In addition, I personally know a couple of people I'd call enlightened and you may be able to think of the name of your personal guru or someone in history you consider to be just that. I'm not saying it doesn't exist, what I'm wary of is the pursuit of it.

Rather, **I'm in favor of ending all the seeking, the never-ending self-improvement, and pursuit of perfection as prerequisites for getting on with it.**

I think seeking enlightenment is a rotten idea if it means:

- Looking for answers, when we are much, much better off with questions.
- Grabbing for proof, when we are better served by not-knowing.
- Striving for a state we feel we are not in, when a state of peace is available to us right now.

We can't let spiritual inquiry, or self-inquiry become a quest for a better ego.

I suggest that the part of us that knows a peaceful state is available to us right now, doesn't think it needs to get enlightened.

I reckon that if you are reading this and you are already enlightened, you might very well agree.

Author's Note
Yun-Men[43] quote from an Anthology of Sacred Prose as edited by Stephen Mitchell in the book "The Enlightened Mind." (Mitchell, 1993)

Originally published as Pair #38 on 05/25/2010

To comment or read other comments online go to:
http://www.elesecoit.com/5/post/2010/05/if-you-see-the-enlightened-one-run.html

---

Oh, Behave!

We all want to be better.

It's a common thing in self-help and in therapy today to offer a variety of ways to be better - which actually boil down to not "being" better so much as just "doing" better.

"Chose!"
"Decide!"
"Manifest!"
"Line Up!"
are all about doing better.

If you pick up a book to help you out with your desire to change it might tell you that you "are" a certain way. For example, maybe you'll be labeled a victim, a reactor ... as opposed to a leader, an owner. You are encouraged to choose the better of the two and chose quickly. Don't "be" this way any more!

Yet this is behavioral change is going to require you to keep a close eye on your daily picks, managing what you think and how you act, watching what you do in order to measure how you are doing at being the new and improved you.

After the time I've spent working with clients (and also for myself) I've become exclusively interested in another kind of change. A change that is easy, natural, positive and lasting, precisely because it does not take effort to sustain.

Don't get me wrong. Changing behaviors is perfectly helpful. I prefer that to nothing. Luckily though, I don't have to choose between that and nothing.

What I've learned, especially through my work with the Three Principles,[44] is that our behaviors follow our emotions and our emotions are the direct product of our thinking.

So whenever we are doing anything we are only ever as good, behaviorally speaking, as the quality of our own thinking in the moment.

In this paradigm, victimhood is an outcome, not a personality type. It is the outcome of a decision that is based on the quality of my thinking at any given time.

For example, if you call me and I answer, "Hello?" and the first words out of your mouth are "What the hell is wrong with you! Why do you do this to me every time?!!!"

I might react in a number of ways.

Indignant, angry, and reactive all spring to mind! After all, the egregious perpetrator has made me his victim in only two short bursts. Right?

Well, this DID happen to me and I really learned something. I heard the words and the anger and I was surprised and curious to see that my reaction was ... connection. "Oh my, I thought, he must be having a really bad day today."

Now, I'm no saint. I'm perfectly capable of as many reactions as anyone. So how did this happen? Was I having a particularly good day? Was I meditating at the time and deeply serene?

Not really. I just heard differently. I heard a human being speaking to me and it was obvious: He was in pain.

This is no behavioral change.

It is a change in behavior brought about by a new level of understanding, new grounding or "beingness" in me. From there I responded in that moment.

This feeling of connection did not come from my advanced training in listening and reflecting back. It did not come from my positive affirmations.

It was a simple moment when, literally without thinking, I was simply part of the dance. I was witnessing the ups and downs of all humans when we are caught up in our thinking and it was fine.

I understood we are only doing as well as we can given our thinking. And that is not a place of pity that is a place of deep, natural connection.

And I realize this is very likely our most natural state. Not a learned one.

So all relationships improve, not when we choose to behave better, but when we focus more on our own deeper understanding of the nature of life.

Author's Note
I've done so much in my life to try to learn to be better and in particular to be able to perform better. Much of what I thought would help me improve both behavior and performance turned out to be wrong.

For those interested in truly understanding what creates high levels of human performance, read Garret Kramer's "Stillpower" (Kramer, 2011) *and listen to the show with Garret*

http://www.elesecoit.com/1/post/2012/02/stillpower-the-inner-source-of-excellence.html

and this show on the single differentiating factor behind human performance
http://elesecoit.com/1/post/2011/09/the-single-biggest-factor-in-human-performance.html

---

Originally published as Pair #99 on 07/01/2011

To comment or read other comments online go to:
http://elesecoit.com/5/post/2011/07/the-recipe-for-better-everything.html

---

Peaceful Includes Not Peaceful

Turbulence Ahead on the Road to Bliss

As humans we all want to be happy. The spiritual journey is often that special search for happiness and well-being that we undertake when all the other searches have failed.

But if you are seated in the last resort spiritual life raft, what do you do if that journey is just as bumpy as all the rest?

Here you are working hard at improving yourself, doing the best you know and then ... you wake up down in the dumps, you yell at your kid, one way or another the halo slips off and with it goes your equilibrium. And your faith.

Now what?

A client recently sheepishly admitted to me he was going through a very dark time and was wondering how it's possible to know so much, be striving every day to put this knowledge to work, be immersed in spiritual teachings and guidance, books, audios, inspirational messages and workshops and still have a bad day. Several actually. Well, OK, a couple of months.

He ended up thinking: "If this spiritual stuff is all about living from a persistent and reliable state of well-being and contentment, how come I'm doing such a bad job of it?"

Who wouldn't draw a similar conclusion? And yet what's happening when we ask "What's wrong with me?" is not just that we are *looking in* the wrong place for an answer, we are *looking from* the wrong place.

Like my client, every one of us who is trying very hard to be better and do better, eventually find themselves in the middle of a down day.

And everything looks bad from there.

In fact it is from the middle of the poo pile that the answer is always going to be the same: "Get me the heck out of here!" That's the only thing you could conclude from the center of your own bad feelings.

So give yourself a break.

If I'm depressed and feeling low, that is when I have the least amount of access to my way out. I am looking at my problem from inside the problem. From the middle of my poor thinking, of course it is going to look like my spiritual understanding is of no use to me. I could conclude all kinds of things about me as a person, a mother, or a friend.

However, **when I am looking at any problem from the larger picture of my life, the bigger truth is that it is not that imperative that this moment be different.** The moment just is. There is nothing permanent about now.

It is as if I'm measuring the each moment as I go and asking, like a kid from the backseat, "Are we THERE yet?!"

I've already set it up as a someday proposition. I'm measuring my progress to destination based on whether I am problem free, always happy, never disappointed, never angry and so on.

What my client and I reflected on together is that perhaps peace of mind is not so much that we always feel peaceful (as somewhere to get to) but rather that when we are not peaceful it's actually OK. It's just not the best place from which to see my problem or my solution clearly.

So we thought it might be true that...

Peacefulness can include "not peaceful."

Peacefulness isn't a good measure of how far we are along our way on the journey to bliss. Peacefulness is the measure of the extent to which we understand how human functioning operates in the big picture.

How it really operates is that we all came here already knowing how to love, how to feel joy, and having an intelligence to use in life. Nothing can ever take that away. No bad moment or bad feeling, no matter how bad, can ever change that.

I personally don't feel peaceful and in my well-being in every single moment — and my single biggest spiritual learning so far is: *this is fine*.

We do a lot of striving in order to feel good *24/7*, when in fact feeling good might just include feeling fine about not always feeling good.

Might as well relax, then.

Author's Note
The nature of change is always inside-out.

For more on this topic...
http://elesecoit.com/2/post/2011/12/what-is-the-inside-out-approach-to-change.html

If you'd like to explore this more, I publish a weekly article on the website and by email called "Well Within: The Inner Sherpa"
http://elesecoit.com/well-within-eleses-blog.html

Originally published as Pair #100 on 07/05/2011

To comment or read other comments online go to:
http://www.elesecoit.com/5/post/2011/07/peaceful-includes-not-peaceful.html

---

The END of Self Improvement

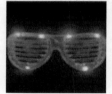

Knock, Knock. Who's there?

There is a wonderful story that was told by Ramana Maharshi[45] (Maharshi, 2004) that goes:

Ten foolish men forded a stream.

On reaching the other shore they wanted to make sure that all of them had in fact safely crossed the stream. So one of the ten began to count, but while counting left himself out.

"I see only nine; sure enough we have lost one! Who can it be?"

"Did you count correctly?" asked another and proceeding to do the counting himself. But he too counted only nine.

One after the other, each of the ten counted only nine, missing himself.

"We are only nine," they agreed, "but who is the missing one?" Every effort they made to discover the missing one failed and so they agreed, surely he had drowned. "Whoever be he who has drowned," said the most sentimental of the foolish ones, "we have lost him." And in so saying, burst into tears.

The rest followed suit.

Seeing them weeping on the riverbank, a sympathetic wayfarer inquired for the cause. They related what had happened and said that even after counting several times they could find no more than nine.

Seeing all the ten before him, the wayfarer guessed what had happened.

Devising a way to make them know for themselves what had happened he placed them in a line and said, "I shall strike each of you so that you may be sure of being included in the count and included only once, upon which you shall count sequentially 'one,' then 'two,' then 'three' and so on. The tenth missing man will then be found."

Hearing this, they rejoiced and accepted the method suggested by the wayfarer.

While the kind wayfarer gave a blow to each of the men, he then counted himself aloud. "Ten," said the last man as he got his blow in turn.

Bewildered, they looked at one another. "We ARE ten," they said with one voice and thanked the wayfarer for having removed their grief.

That is the parable. And so it is for us.

We are unhappy and we begin to look for change. We look for a better and improved self. We look for an authentic self. We look and look and look.

I can identify with this story having spent many years now looking for some version of myself I hoped would be an improvement on the old model: More successful, wealthier, happier.

I saw self-development as something that went forwards, onwards and, if I was lucky, read enough or worked hard enough, it would go steadily upwards.

Culminating in what? A better me? An awakened me? The New Me!

There isn't a program out there to help that isn't promising some form of a new you.

What I've come to see is that the only reason I'm unhappy with the current me is that I've forgotten who I am.

I'll let Maharshi close this series of 101 Pairs of Glasses.

He just says it so well:

"You yourself impose limitations on your true nature of Infinite Being and then weep that you are but a finite creature...

I say know that you are really the infinite, pure Being, the Self Absolute. You are always that Self and nothing but that Self. Therefore, you can never be really ignorant of the Self.

True Knowledge does not create a new Being for you; it only removes your 'ignorant ignorance.' Bliss is not added to your nature; it is merely revealed as your true and natural state."

Author's notes:
All Ramana Maharshi quotes from The Spiritual Teachings of Ramana Maharshi, Foreword by C G Jung, Shambala Classics (Maharshi, 2004).

Originally published as Pair #101 on 07/12/2011

To comment or read other comments online go to:
http://elesecoit.com/5/post/2011/07/the-end-of-self-improvement.html

The appearance of things change according to the emotions
and thus we see magic and beauty in them,
while the magic and beauty are really in ourselves.
Kahlil Gilbran

Bibliography and Resources

Baer, G. (2003). *Real Love.* New York: Penguin.

Banks, S. (1998). *The Mising Link.* Canada: Lone Pine.

Chandler, S. *The Story of You.* Franklin Lakes: Career Press.

Christian Science. (2011). Retrieved from http://www.spirituality.com

Coit, L. (2010). *Awakening.* CA: Las Brisas.

de Mello, A. (1992). *Awareness.* Doubleday.

Evans, M. (1990). *Travelling Free: How to Recover from the Past by Changing Your Beliefs.* Desert Hot Springs: Yes You Can Press.

Fenner, P. (2007). *Radiant Mind.* Canada: Sounds True.

Frankl, V. E. (2006). *Man's Search For Meaning.* Boston: Beacon Press.

Goldsmith, J. (1962). *Conscious Union With God.* Secaucus: Citadel.

Holden, R. (2009). *Be Happy.* Carlsbad: Hay House.

Katie, B. (2005). *I Need Your Love, Is That True?* New York: Three Rivers.

Kramer, G. (2011). *Stillpower.* Austin: Green Leaf.

Krznaric, R. (2011). *The Wonderbox: Curious Histories of How to Live.* London: Profile Books.

Louden, J. (2005). *Woman's Comfort Book: A Self-Nurturing Guide for Restoring Balance in Your Life.* New York: HarperOne.

Maharshi, R. (2004). *The Spiritual Teachings of Ramana Maharshi.* Boston: Shambala Classics.

Mitchell, S. (1993). *The Enlightened Mind.* NY: Harper Perennial .

Neill, M. (2009). *Supercoach.* Hay House.

Pransky, G. (2001). *The Relationship Handbook*. La Conner: Pransky and Associates.

Pressfield, S. (2011). *The War of Art*. New York city: Black Irish Entertainment LLC.

Rachel Naomi Remen, M. (2000). *My Grandfather's Blessings*. New York: Riverhead Books.

Roshi, G. (2007). *Big Mind – Big Heart: Finding Your Way*. Mclean, VA: Big Mind Publishing.

Stanier, M. B. (2010). *Do More Great Work*. New York: Workman Publishing.

Sterner, T. (2012). *The Practicing Mind, Developing Focus and Discipline In Your Life*. Wilmington, CA, Novato: New World Library.

Taylor, E. (2010). InnerTalk Newsletter /What Does That Mean? 10-20. Carlsbad, Ca, USA: Hay House.

Taylor, E. (2009). *Mind Programming*. Carlsbad, CA: Hay Houe.

Index

About The Author

Elese Coit, Expert in Human Potential
Leader in Transformative Personal and Organizational Change

 Elese is an expert on the human factor in leadership, management and business performance. Formerly a senior corporate manager, she now travels widely to consult, speak and coach. Blending her business savvy with the principles of human transformation, she helps organizations and individuals to elevate performance, wellbeing and potential in a way that is sustainable and self-propagating.

Elese is a Certified Master Transformative Coach and a trainer of coaches. One of her passions is to spread the inside-out paradigm for transformative change to the coaching profession. Her life mission is to assist other difference-makers to make an even bigger difference.

Elese also hosts the highly acclaimed international radio show "A New Way To Handle Absolutely Everything" and continues to write books, articles and blogs exploring the nature of the human experience and vastness of our human potential. Through her work and radio show Elese has made a difference to hundreds of thousands of lives around the globe.

Alongside her organizational seminars, trainings and retreats, Elese offers professional development for coaches as well as occasional public classes on topics such as wellbeing, stress reduction and relationships. She accepts a small number of private clients each year for one-on-one transformative coaching.

See **www.elesecoit.com** to find out more about her books and classes or to hire Elese for coaching, training or speaking engagements.

To contact Elese directly send her an email at: elese@elesecoit.com

To stay up to date with the most recent distinctions in the fields of Transformative Change and Wellness, subscribe to "Well Within" and get the latest article sent to you by email. See Elese's home page for how to sign up and claim the gifts available to subscribers.

End Notes

[1] www.innertalk.com

[2] www.stevechandler.com

[3] www.supercoachacademy.com

[4] www.sirkenrobinson.com

[5] www.demello.org

[6] www.germaneconsulting.com

[7] www.jacobglass.com

[8] www.supercoach.com

[9] www.huffingtonpost.com

[10] www.thefluentself.com

[11] www.uncommon-knowledge.co.uk/articles/making-decisions.html

[12] www.news.stanford.edu/news/2009/august24/multitask-research-study-082409.html

[13] www.oneperson.net

[14] www.leecoit.com

[15] www.servicetoself.com

[16] www.pranskyandassociates.com

[17] www.mandyevans.com

[18] www.kristinnoelle.com/2011/05/18/do-you-need-your-butt-kicked

[19] www.radiantmind.com

[20] www.thework.com

[21] www.kevinlaye.co.uk

[22] www.christianscience.com

[23] www.healthrealize.com

[24] www.robertholden.org

[25] www.barbarsher.com

[26] www.Augustturak.com

[27] www.kristinecarlson.com

[28] www.jenniferlouden.com

[29] www.rachelremen.com

[30] www.mysticalmama.com

[31] www.outrospection.org and www.romankrznaric.com

[32] www.centerforsustainablechange.org

[33] www.boxofcrayons.biz

[34] www.billyconnolly.com

[35] www.rickhanson.net

[36] www.mysticcool.com

[37] www.clubfearless.net

[38] www.reallove.com

[39] www.en.wikipedia.org/wiki/Ogden_Nash

[40] www.alicampbell.com

[41] www.acim.org

[42] www.bigmind.org

[43] www.stephenmitchellbooks.com/anthologies/enlightenedMind.html

[44] An overview of The Three Principles: www.centerforsustainablechange.org/principles.php

[45] Ramana Maharshi at www.shambhala.com/html/catalog/items/isbn/978-1-59030-139-5.cfm

13219496R00131

Printed in Great Britain
by Amazon.co.uk, Ltd.,
Marston Gate.